FIRST FUN ENCYCLOPEDIA

First published in 2001 by Miles Kelly Publishing Ltd
Bardfield Centre
Great Bardfield
Essex CM7 4SL

2 4 6 8 1 0 9 7 5 3

This edition printed 2002

British Library Cataloguing-in-Publication Data
A catalogue record for this book is available from the British Library

ISBN 1-902947-85-1

Printed in Hong Kong

Author
Jane Walker

Editorial Director
Paula Borton

Project Management
Belinda Gallagher

Editorial Assistant
Mark Darling

Copy Editor
Ann Kay

Proofreader
Margaret Berrill

Art Director
Clare Sleven

Designer
David Gillingwater

Consultants
Peter Riley
Philip Steele

www.mileskelly.net
info@mileskelly.net

FIRST
FUN
ENCYCLOPEDIA

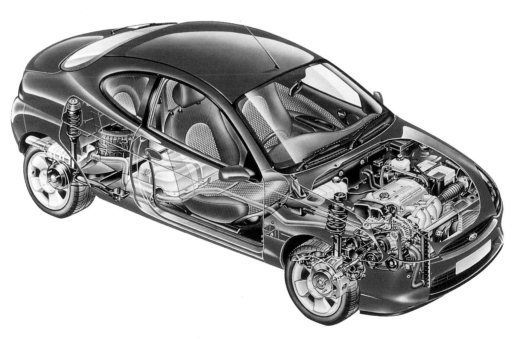

Jane Walker

Miles Kelly

PUBLISHING

Contents

How to use this book

Your *First Fun Encyclopedia* is bursting with information, colour pictures and fun things to do. The pages run from A to Z with a new subject on every page. This will help you find information quickly and easily. There are comic cartoons to bring amazing true facts to life and puzzles and games to tease your brain. The index at the back of the book will help you look for specific information.

Colour bands

Your encyclopedia has six subject areas. The coloured bands along the top of each page tell you which subject area you are in.
History has red bands.
Natural World has orange bands.
People and Places has green bands.
Planet Earth has purple bands.
Science has blue bands.
Universe has yellow bands.

Pictures

Illustrations or photographs accompany each caption. Many illustrations are labelled to explain what different parts of them are called.

Wow boxes

Look for the orange panels to read amazing true facts – the funny cartoons will make you laugh!

Alphabet strip

Your book is alphabetical. This means it runs from A to Z. Along the bottom of every page is an alphabet strip. The letter that starts the main heading is in bold. Above the letter there's a small arrow to highlight where you are in the alphabet.

Pollution

Litter in the street, dirty smoke and gases in the air, dangerous chemicals in rivers and streams – all these are examples of pollution. Pollution is the waste products that damage the air, the land and the water around us. It can kill plants and animals, make humans beings ill and even damage old buildings.

Word b

soot
the black powde
smoke from a c

transpo
to move from o
to anoth

▲ Oil disaster

Oil is transported across the sea by tankers. Sometimes a tanker is involved in an accident, leading to an oil spillage. This can have a devastating effect, killing marine life for miles around. Oil is also washed up on beaches, and cleaning up can take months, even years.

► Into the water

All over the world, people pour harmful waste into streams, lakes and rivers. This water pollution kills fish and the water plants they feed on, and makes the water unsafe for people to drink.

▲ Dirty air

The gases from car exhausts fill our cities with soot, smoke and other dirt. This dirty air can harm people's eyes and make it difficult for them to breathe. By using cleaner fuel, people can help to reduce the level of polluted air.

▼ Using ag

We can reduce the a
waste from our hom
it. Recycling means t
product into
another material
and using it
again. You
can recycle
glass bottles
and jars,
newspapers
and
cardboard,
drinks and
food cans,
plastic bottles
and old clothing.

Wow!
If we recycled three-quarters of all the paper in the world, we would save more than 35 million trees every year.

Main text
Every page begins with a paragraph of main text to each subject.

Cross-references
Within the colour band are cross-references to other subjects. These tell you where you can find more information about your chosen topic. Follow the arrows to turn backwards or forwards to the correct page.

Prehistoric life

Find out more:
Art and painting ◄ Dinosaurs ◄

Word boxes
New or difficult words are explained in the yellow panels.

The first human beings lived on Earth a long time ago – around 2 million years ago. At this time most of the world was cold and icy, but Africa, South America and parts of Asia were warmer. These early people learned how to make fire, hunted animals and made simple tools from wood, stone and animal bones.

Word box

bison
huge prehistoric cattle

prehistoric
the time before history was written down

▼ A long time ago

The word 'prehistoric' means the time before people could write. It is the time before about 5,000 years ago. This period of prehistory is called the Stone Age. People made their own tools and weapons out of stone.

woolly mammoth

Captions
Captions give you detailed information about all the photographs and illustrations in your book.

▲ Making fire

The earliest use of fire-making was for warmth. But people eventually discovered the uses of fire – for cooking, to shape weapons and tools, and to give light.

this stone tool was used for scraping flesh from the skin of wild animals

▲ Mammoth hunts

Early people hunted birds, small reptiles and larger animals such as deer, bison, bears and huge elephant-like animals called woolly mammoths.

Animal match

These prehistoric animals are either mammals, reptiles or amphibians. See if you can tell what they are.

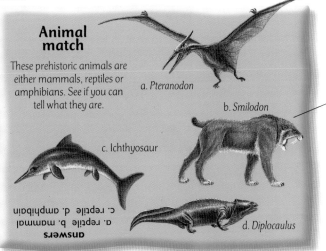
a. Pteranodon
b. Smilodon
c. Ichthyosaur
d. Diplocaulus

answers
a. reptile b. mammal c. reptile d. amphibian

▲ Cave art

Prehistoric people painted pictures of animals and everyday life on cave walls. The first person to find any of these pictures was a 12-year-old Spanish girl, more than 100 years ago.

Activity and puzzle boxes
Some pages will have activities, games or puzzles for you to do. Look for the green, blue and purple panels.

Africa

Find out more:
African people ▶ Deserts ▶ Grasslands ▶

Africa is the second largest continent in the world, after Asia. It is a land of great contrasts, with hot deserts, thick forests and grassy plains. Most places are either hot and wet, or hot and dry. The world's longest river, the Nile, flows through North Africa to the east of the biggest desert in the world, the Sahara.

▶ Amazing sights

Africa is a land of spectacular sights, including the Great Rift Valley and the towering Mount Kilimanjaro, shown here, which is the remains of an extinct volcano.

▼ Victoria Falls

The Victoria Falls are situated on the border between Zambia and Zimbabwe. Local people call them the 'smoke that thunders' because they make a deafening noise and produce a smoke-like spray of mist.

▶ Hunters and hunted

Animals such as giraffes and antelopes roam across the African grasslands, followed by hunters such as lions. They all share the same watering hole.

elephant

giraffe

buffalo

warthog

hippopotamus

antelope

lion

African people

Find out more:
Africa ◄ Deserts ► Grasslands ► Prehistoric life ►

Most of Africa's population lives south of the Sahara Desert. The people of North Africa are mainly Arabs. Farther south, the people can be divided into more than 800 different groups, each with its own way of life and often its own language.

▲ Busy cities

Although more than half the population live in small villages, Africa has some large, bustling cities. Cairo, the capital of Egypt, is one of the busiest.

▲ Life in the desert

The Tuareg people come from the Sahara Desert. Traditionally they are nomads, people who move from place to place in search of fresh grazing for their camels, goats, sheep and cattle.

▼ Which foods?

In the hot, wet parts of West Africa farmers grow bananas, coconuts, cassava, rice, cocoa and tea.

▼ Nelson Mandela

Nelson Mandela was the first black president of South Africa (1994–99). As a young man he fought for the rights of black South Africans. White leaders imprisoned him for his beliefs for 28 years (1962–90).

Word box

cassava
a thick root that is cooked and eaten like a potato

nomads
people who do not settle in one place, moving from area to area

Air

Find out more:
Plants ▶ Pollution ▶

Air is the mixture of gases that you breathe. You cannot see, smell or taste air but it is all around you. Layers of air surround our planet Earth, too, making up the Earth's 'atmosphere'. Oxygen is a gas found in the air. All animals, including humans, need it to stay alive.

▶ Oxygen-makers

Animals take in oxygen from the air and breathe out a waste gas called carbon dioxide. Plants do the opposite. They take carbon dioxide from the air and turn it into oxygen. The oxygen is given off through their leaves.

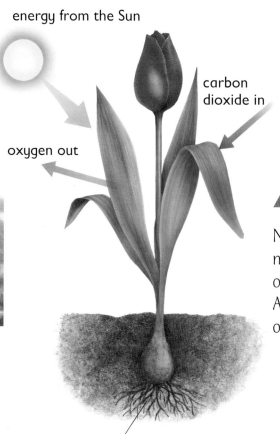

energy from the Sun

carbon dioxide in

oxygen out

roots

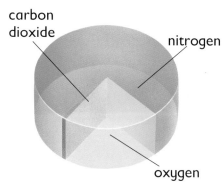

carbon dioxide

nitrogen

oxygen

▲ Gases in air

Nitrogen and oxygen are the two main gases in air. About one-fifth of the air you breathe is oxygen. Air also contains tiny amounts of a gas called carbon dioxide.

▲ Moving air

When the wind blows it is really air on the move. If you stand outside on a windy day you can feel this flowing air as it rushes past you.

Wow!

On calm days a thick, yellow fog called smog hangs over the American city of Los Angeles. It is mainly caused by exhaust gases from traffic.

▶ Dirty air

Traffic fumes, dust and various other specks in the air can cause an illness called asthma. People with asthma often have to use special sprays to help them breathe more easily.

Amphibians

Frogs, toads, newts and salamanders are amphibians. Most amphibians are small animals with soft, smooth skins. They can live on land as well as in water and are found near ponds, streams and lakes. Amphibians usually breed in water.

▶ Lots of amphibians

There are more than 3,500 different kinds of amphibian. The largest is the Japanese giant salamander, shown here, which is more than 1.5 metres long. Newts are very like salamanders, but in general, they spend more of their lives in water.

Japanese giant salamander

◀ Poisonous frogs

Frogs and toads make up the biggest group of amphibians. This poison arrow frog lives in the rainforests of South America. Its poisonous skin helps to protect it from enemies.

▼ From egg to frog

Tiny tadpoles hatch in water from the eggs of a female frog. As they grow, tadpoles develop four legs and a frog-like body. After a few months the tadpole has changed into a frog.

▼ Greedy toad

The cane toad is a pest. It was introduced to Australia in the 1930s to eat beetles. Unfortunately it also began to eat other frogs, lizards and birds living in the area!

cane toad

1. the female frog lays hundreds of soft eggs (spawn) in the water

2. the tadpoles hatch from the eggs

3. the tadpoles grow legs and change into froglets

4. the froglet loses its tail and changes into a frog

Animal kingdom

Find out more:
Amphibians ◄ Animal life ► Birds ► Fish ► Insects ►
Mammals ► Reptiles ► Spiders and their relatives ►

Animals live in almost every corner of the world. They swim in the oceans, walk or run across the land, and fly through the air. The biggest animal on land, the African elephant, weighs as much as a farm tractor. You need a microscope to see the smallest animals.

there are five main kinds of **vertebrates**:

birds

amphibians

mammals

fish

reptiles

► Animal groups

We divide animals into two main groups: vertebrates (animals with backbones) and invertebrates (animals without backbones). Within each group there are many kinds of animal. For example, roundworms and sponges are two different kinds of invertebrate.

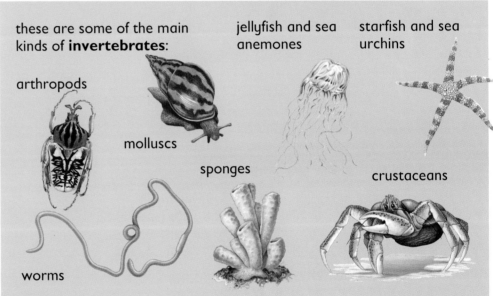

these are some of the main kinds of **invertebrates**:

jellyfish and sea anemones

starfish and sea urchins

arthropods

molluscs

sponges

crustaceans

worms

▼ Biggest of all

The blue whale is the biggest animal on Earth. A male can weigh as much as 120 tonnes and be up to 26 metres in length.

◄ Lots of insects

Insects are the biggest group of animals. There are more than one million different kinds. All insects have six legs, and most can fly.

Wow!

Some large land tortoises can live to be around 200 years old.

Animal life

Find out more:
Amphibians ◄ Animal kingdom ◄ Fish ► Insects ► Mammals ►
Reptiles ► Spiders and their relatives ►

Animals live in hot deserts and on snowy mountain-tops, in thick jungles and on open grasslands. Where an animal or group of animals lives is called a habitat. For example, the hot rainforest of South America is the habitat of jaguars, monkeys and parrots. The frozen land of Antarctica is the habitat of penguins.

▶ Working animals

Across the world, people and animals work together to do different jobs.

in Asia, elephants carry loads

sheep dogs are used all over the world to round up sheep

in India, oxen pull ploughs

▼ In the cold

Polar bears can survive on the frozen land and in the icy cold waters of the Arctic. Their thick coat of fur protects them from the cold. A thick layer of fat below the skin also helps to keep them warm.

▲ Hot and dry

a large surface area from which body heat is lost

Animals that live in very hot places, such as the fennec fox, often have long ears and tails to help their bodies lose heat.

▼ Animal travellers

Some animals travel huge distances to look for warmer weather or food supplies each year. This journey is called a migration. In North America, caribou travel thousands of kilometres to find food in winter.

▼ Animals and sport

For thousands of years, people have trained horses to take part in races. Races between horse-drawn chariots were held in ancient Rome. Horse races have been held in Europe since the early 1600s.

Antarctica

Find out more:
Explorers ▶ World ▶

Antarctica is the world's coldest continent. This bare, icy land lies around the South Pole, the most southerly place on the Earth. Most of Antarctica is covered with a huge sheet of ice which is up to three kilometres thick in places. During winter, Antarctica is completely dark because the Sun never rises there.

• South Pole

◀ Land of ice and snow

Huge chunks break off the ice around the South Pole to form icebergs, which float out to sea. Icebergs are a danger to ships.

Roald Amundsen

◀ Race to the South Pole

Many explorers tried to reach the South Pole after people first sighted Antarctica in 1820. In 1911 two teams of explorers, one from Norway and one from Great Britain, began a race to the South Pole. The team led by Norwegian Roald Amundsen arrived first.

▶ A cold life

Only a few land animals, such as penguins, can survive the freezing conditions of Antarctica. Yet the waters of the Antarctic Ocean are filled with seals, fish, squid and tiny, shrimp-like creatures called krill. Several kinds of whale spend the summer months in Antarctica.

young emperor penguins rely on their parents for food and warmth

Art and painting

Early humans first painted pictures of animals on cave walls about 30,000 years ago. A great deal of early art was created for gods and religion. Since that time, people everywhere have produced all kinds of painting, sculpture, carving and pottery – we call them works of art.

▲ Kinds of paint

Different kinds of paint produce different effects. Oil paints are thick and textured. Watercolours (above) are much thinner and softer.

▶ Artists at work

Some artists paint pictures onto the walls or ceiling of a building. An Italian artist called Michelangelo took four years to paint the ceiling of the Sistine Chapel (right) in Rome. He began in 1508 and finished in 1512. Michelangelo used an effect called *fresco,* which involved painting onto damp, freshly laid plaster.

Fabergé egg

Wow!
Some paintbrushes are so fine that they are made from just one or two hairs. The artists work with a magnifying glass to see what they are doing!

◀ Decorative art

Peter Carl Fabergé was a Russian jeweller, whose decorative art skills became popular with the Russian tsars in the 1880s. He is most famous for his beautifully decorated Easter eggs.

▶ Looking at art

You can visit an art gallery to look at paintings and sculptures. This is the Guggenheim Gallery, in New York, USA.

Asia

Asia is the biggest continent in the world. It stretches from the Mediterranean coast of the Near East, to the islands of Japan, off Asia's eastern coast. A range of mountains called the Himalayas separates the warmer, wetter countries of southern Asia from the rest of the continent.

▶ Highest place on Earth

The world's highest mountain is in Asia – Mount Everest. It is 8,848 metres high. Mount Everest is part of the Himalayas, a mountain range on the border between Nepal and Tibet.

◀ Heavy rain

In southern Asia, winds called monsoons blow at certain times of the year. These winds bring very heavy rains.

▼ Rare wildlife

In the rainforest areas of Borneo and Sumatra lives the orang-utan, the only great ape to live in Asia. It is now a protected species.

▼ Cold desert

The Gobi Desert, in central Asia, is classed as a cold desert. It is a bare, windy place, covered with rocks and sandy soil.

Word box

monsoon
strong winds and heavy rains

range
a line of mountains

tropical
hot, wet conditions

Asian people

Around two-thirds of all the people in the world live in Asia. Most live near rivers or by the coast, where they make a living from farming and fishing. Many people are moving to the cities, where living conditions are often very crowded.

▼ Rice-growing

Nearly two-thirds of the rice in the world is grown in just two Asian countries – China and India. Rice is grown in flooded fields called paddies.

▶ By bike

The streets of Chinese cities are filled with people riding bicycles. The bicycle is the most popular way of getting around in China.

▲ River life

The river Ganges is India's busiest waterway. People come to trade goods, and many bathe in the water, which is believed to be holy.

◀ Following religion

This Buddhist statue is in Thailand. Asian people follow many different religions, including Hinduism, Islam and Buddhism.

▲ Tea trade

Tea is an important crop in Asia. The leaves are taken to nearby factories to be sorted and dried.

Word scramble

Unscramble these words to find the names of five Asian countries:

a. DLINHATA
b. ACNIH
c. TWIKAU
d. LEPAN
e. GLOAMOIN

answers
a. Thailand b. China c. Kuwait d. Nepal e. Mongolia

Babies

A human baby spends about nine months inside its mother's body before being born. It takes about 40 weeks for a baby to grow from a tiny egg to a small human being – with eyes, ears, a nose, fingers and toes.

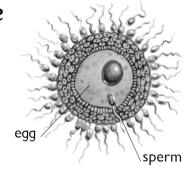

egg

sperm

◀ Life begins

A baby starts out as a tiny egg inside its mother's body. This egg has joined with a tiny cell called a sperm, which comes from the father.

▶ From egg to baby

The egg begins to grow inside its mother's body and it divides quickly into lots of other cells. These cells group together to form different body parts.

at 6 weeks the egg develops quickly and is called an embryo

at 8 weeks the growing embryo is called a foetus

at 12 weeks the foetus looks like a very tiny baby

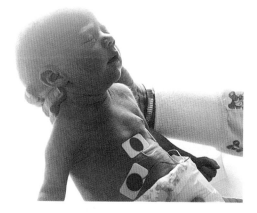

▲ A newborn baby

Newborn babies cannot walk, talk or feed themselves. At first the baby feeds only on milk, either from the mother or from a bottle.

▼ Getting around

In Africa, many mothers carry their babies on their back. The mother has both hands free while the baby is held safely against her body.

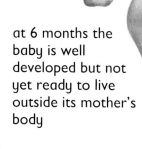

at 6 months the baby is well developed but not yet ready to live outside its mother's body

at 9 months the baby is ready to be born. A newborn baby is about 50 centimetres long

▼ Learning to move

Babies can crawl by eight months. They take their first steps and usually say their first word at about one year old.

Wow!

By the age of six a child knows more than 2,500 different words.

Bicycles

Riding a bicycle is one of the world's most popular ways of travelling from place to place. We use bicycles, or bikes for short, to travel to school or work, to deliver things, to race as a sport and to take exercise. Each bike is specially designed for the job it has to do.

▲ Fast bikes

A racing bike is light to help it travel quickly. It is made of a strong material, such as aluminium, plastic or carbon fibre. The rider changes gear to suit his speed. Thin tyres are also designed for speed.

▼ Mountain bikes

Mountain bikes are strong and chunky so they can move over rough ground. The wide tyres grip well on slippery, uneven surfaces.

▼ Bicycle taxis

In India and other Asian countries, bicycles are used as taxis. They pull two-wheeled carriages where the passengers can sit. These taxis are called rickshaws, and they are also used for moving heavy goods about.

Word box

carbon fibre
a strong, light material made from plastic and threads of carbon

gear
a toothed wheel that helps the cyclist to pedal more easily

▶ Early bikes

The penny farthing was one of the earliest bicycles. The first ones appeared in 1870. Its giant front wheel was about 1.5 metres high. Each time the rider made one complete turn of the pedals, the big wheel turned all the way round.

Birds

Birds are the only animals with feathers. All birds have wings too, but not all birds can fly. Penguins cannot fly but they are good swimmers. The ostrich cannot fly but it can run at speeds of more than 60 kilometres per hour, faster than any other bird.

▼ Making nests

Most birds lay their eggs in nests made inside trees and bushes, on cliff ledges, in riverbanks, or in holes in the ground. The weaver bird makes a complicated nest by knotting strips of leaves together.

large, powerful legs allow the ostrich to travel long distances

the male weaver twists strips of leaves around a branch or twig

he makes a roof and an entrance

the finished nest has a long entrance, and provides safety and shelter for the eggs

◄ Fast and big

Ostriches are the only birds with two toes. This means that less of their foot makes contact with the ground, which makes them fast runners.

▼ Different bills

Birds use their bills, or beaks, to get food and to protect themselves. The bill of the grosbeak is short and fat — ideal for eating berries and seeds.

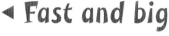

▼ Long-distance traveller

Some birds leave their home during winter to find food in warmer places. This journey is called migration. The Arctic tern flies more than 17,000 kilometres from its summer home in the Arctic to the Antarctic in the south.

▼ Breaking out

Many baby birds are blind and helpless when they break out of their shells. They are cared for by their parents for several weeks.

the chick chips at the egg

the egg begins to crack

the egg splits open

the chick wriggles out

Birds of the world

There are more than 8,000 different kinds of bird. The largest is the African ostrich, which can grow to be taller than a man. The smallest is the bee hummingbird, which could easily fit in the palm of your hand. Birds live in every corner of the world, from hot deserts to the icy lands of Antarctica.

bee hummingbird

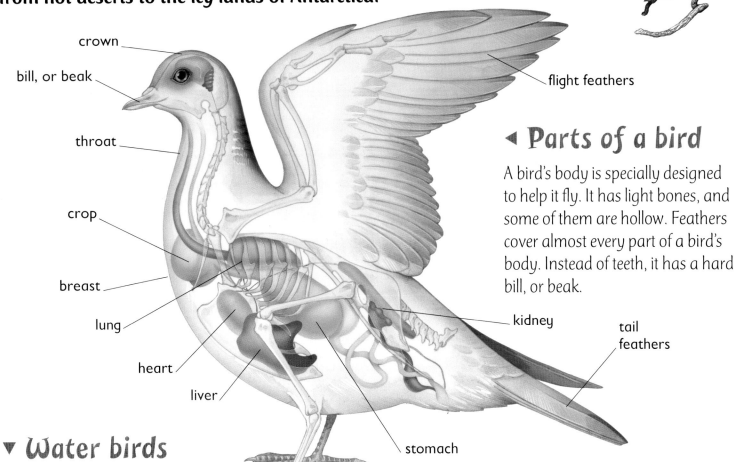

crown
bill, or beak
throat
crop
breast
lung
heart
liver
toes
stomach
flight feathers
kidney
tail feathers

◀ Parts of a bird

A bird's body is specially designed to help it fly. It has light bones, and some of them are hollow. Feathers cover almost every part of a bird's body. Instead of teeth, it has a hard bill, or beak.

▼ Water birds

Puffins live on cliffs by the sea. They dive into the water to catch fish. Their large beaks enable them to hold many fish at once

▶ Birds of prey

Birds that are fierce hunters of other animals are called birds of prey. They include eagles, vultures, hawks and owls. They have sharp claws and strong, sharp bills. This owl is hunting a mouse.

Books

Millions of new books are created every year.
Some, like this encyclopedia, have both words and pictures
in them. Some books have only words, some have mainly
pictures and very few words. We read books to give us
information as well as for enjoyment.

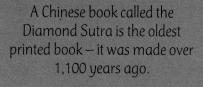

Wow!

A Chinese book called the
Diamond Sutra is the oldest
printed book – it was made over
1,100 years ago.

▼ Story time

This library contains thousands
of different books. We borrow
books from libraries to take home
and read.

▼ Printing books

The first book ever printed in
English was produced by William
Caxton, an English printer, in 1474.
Caxton's printing press was one of
the first of its kind. Altogether,
Caxton printed about 100 books.

▼ Writing books

Charles Dickens (1812–1870) wrote
some of the most famous books in
world literature. His characters were
brought to life in classics such as
Oliver Twist, *A Christmas Carol* and
David Copperfield.

▲ Made by hand

Before printing was invented,
people made books by hand. This
work was often done by monks.
They copied out the words and then
decorated each page with colourful
illustrations and borders.

▼ Book characters

We all have favourite characters
from the books we
have read. How
many of these
famous book
characters
do you
recognize?

Word box

illustrations
the pictures in a book

monk
a religious man who lives
a simple life

Buildings

A concrete skyscraper, a hut of clay bricks, a pyramid of steel and glass and a red-brick house – all these are different kinds of building. The style of a building depends on how it will be used, what the climate is like and which building materials are available.

▲ Using materials

The Dayak people of Malaysia build houses from bamboo, called longhouses. They are built on tall poles to keep them dry when the land is flooded.

▼ Domed shape

The Millennium Dome in London is the biggest domed building in Europe. It was built specially to celebrate the start of year 2000.

▲ Skyscrapers

A huge skyscraper usually has a frame of steel or concrete. The windows and the walls, which are made of concrete, steel or glass, are attached to this frame.

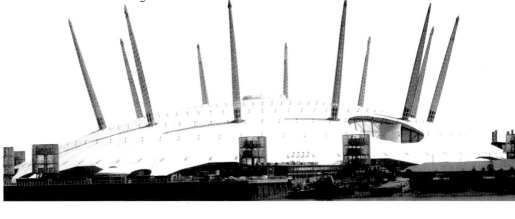

▼ Old buildings

The Great Pyramids in Egypt were built 4,500 years ago as tombs for Egyptian kings and queens. The pyramids are still standing, but some are partly in ruins.

Wow!

The tallest self-supporting building in the world is the CN Tower in Toronto, Canada. It stands at 553 metres tall, more than five times taller than the Statue of Liberty in New York, USA!

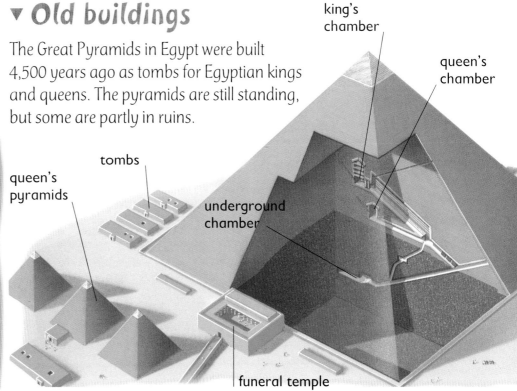

king's chamber

queen's chamber

tombs

queen's pyramids

underground chamber

funeral temple

Cars

Today, there are more than 500 million motor cars on the world's roads. They come in many different shapes and sizes, from small three-wheeled ones to large four-wheel drive cars for travelling over rough ground. Most cars are powered by an engine, which burns either petrol or diesel fuel.

Wow!

The longest car in the world is so long, it has a swimming pool inside it!

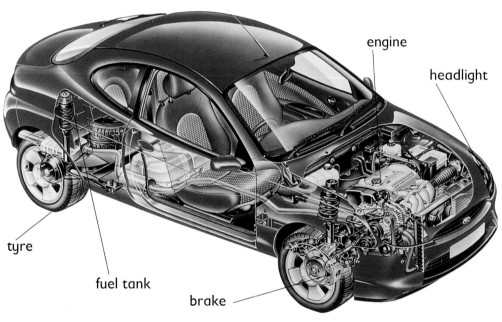

engine

headlight

tyre

fuel tank

brake

▲ Parts of a car

A car has thousands of different parts. This cutaway view shows some of the most important ones.

▲ Cleaner cars

Electric cars are cleaner because they do not produce waste gases like cars that use petrol or diesel. Waste gases from motor cars pollute the air.

▼ Motor racing

Racing cars have a sleek shape to help them go faster. This Formula One racing car can reach speeds of up to 320 kilometres per hour.

Word box

mass-produced
made in large numbers

pollute
make dirty

sleek
smooth and shiny

▲ Early cars

One of the earliest mass-produced cars was the Model T, built by the Ford company in the United States. For about 20 years it was the most popular car and over 15 million of them were sold during this time.

Castles

A castle is a strong building that protects the people who live inside it. Most castles are built from stone, although the first ones were wooden. Castles were mainly built in countries in Europe during a time known as the Middle Ages, around AD900 to 1500.

▶ Life in a castle

The centre of castle life was the keep, where the lord of the castle and his family lived. Castles were usually surrounded by a high outer wall, and often a water-filled ditch called a moat.

▲ Crusader knights

In the Middle Ages, Christian knights from Europe travelled to the Near East to fight the Muslims. They were known as crusader knights. They built hilltop castles to defend themselves.

▶ Under attack!

Attackers used huge machines called siege engines to break down a castle's defences. During a siege the attacking side would try to stop supplies of food and water from reaching the people inside the castle.

bailey   keep   battlements

gatehouse   drawbridge   portcullis   moat

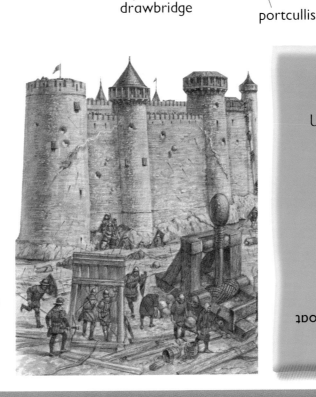

Word scramble

Unscramble these words to find the names of five important parts of a castle:

a. peke
b. stroplucil
c. yilabe
d. outhesage
e. atom

answers
a. keep b. portcullis c. bailey d. gatehouse e. moat

Clothing

Find out more:
Materials ▶

We choose our clothing to suit what we do each day. To play sport we wear hard-wearing but comfortable clothes that let us move freely. In cold weather we wear clothing to keep us warm. In some parts of the world, people still wear traditional clothes that they have worn for centuries, particularly in country areas.

▶ Uniforms

A uniform tells you that a person does a certain job, or belongs to an organization. You notice doctors in hospitals from what they are wearing.

Wow!

In ancient Rome, only the emperor was allowed to wear an all-purple toga. A toga was a loose piece of cloth worn by men.

▲ Keeping warm

People who live in cold climates, such as Inuits in the far north, often wear thick layers of clothing made from natural materials such as wool, fur or leather. Scientists have developed new synthetic materials made from chemicals, which are also extremely warm.

▼ Keeping cool

In hot countries, people wear loose-fitting clothing to keep cool. Their clothes are made of cotton or linen. They are usually light-coloured to reflect the Sun's rays.

▼ Clothes for the job

Some workers have to wear special clothing for their job. Fire-fighters wear protective suits made of a material that stops their bodies from being burned.

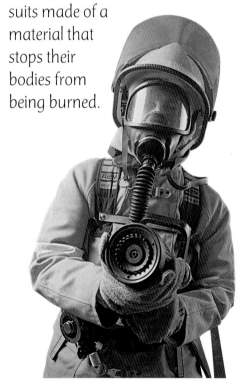

▶ Egyptian dress

Thousands of years ago, people in ancient Egypt wore clothes made of white linen. Men wore long wrap-around skirts, and women wore long straight dresses. Poor people, children and slaves often wore no clothes at all.

Word box

climate
the usual weather of a place over a long period of time

reflect
to make light bounce back

synthetic
not natural

Colour

Colour is all around you – in the clothes you wear, in the flowers in the park, in a rainbow in the sky and on your TV screen. Even the light from the Sun, which seems to have no colour at all, is filled with colour.

► Colours of the rainbow

When white light passes through a glass prism, it breaks up into the different colours of the rainbow: red, orange, yellow, green, blue, indigo and violet.

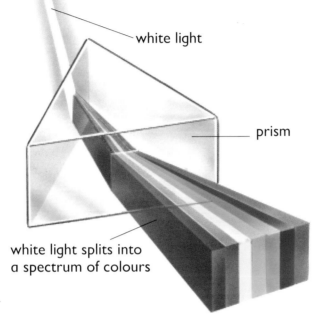

white light

prism

white light splits into a spectrum of colours

a rainbow occurs when raindrops in the air act like prisms

▲ Warning colours

Some animals use colour to warn off their enemies. The bright markings on this butterfly's wings tell its enemies that it tastes nasty!

► Mixing colours

We mix colours together to create different ones. Only three colours of light – red, blue and green – are needed to make all the other colours. These three colours, called primary colours, produce all the pictures that you see on your television screen.

Colour mix

Red, blue and yellow are the primary colours of paint. All other paint colours are made from them. Can you fill in these gaps with the correct colours?

a. red + . . . = orange
b. . . . + red = purple
c. blue + yellow = . . .

answers
a. yellow b. blue c. green

Communication

Find out more:
Computers ▶ Sound and hearing ▶ Spacecraft

Did you write a letter today, make a phone call or send someone a message by e-mail? All these are different ways of communicating with other people. Simple communications use a smile or a wave. More complicated ones use computers and satellites in space.

Word box

e-mail
short for electronic mail (sending letters by computer)

remote
far away

satellite
a spacecraft that circles the Earth

▲ Faraway places

In remote parts of Australia, the only way to communicate with others is by radio. Some children do their schoolwork by talking to their teacher over a two-way radio.

Wow!

There are more telephones than people in the city of Washington D.C., capital of the USA.

▼ First telephone

The first telephone was made in 1876 by a Scottish-born inventor called Alexander Graham Bell.

▼ Up in space

When you telephone someone in a distant country, the signal from your call is beamed up to a satellite above Earth. The satellite then sends the signal through space, back down to the Earth and into the other person's phone.

▼ On the move

With the help of mobile phones, people can keep in touch with each other, wherever they are. These phones are small enough to fit in your pocket — or even in the palm of your hand.

satellite

telephone exchange sends messages along the phone network

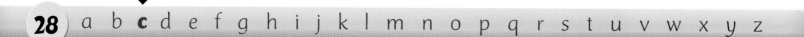

Computers

Find out more:
Electricity ▶

Computers are a part of your daily life – you use them at school and possibly at home too. Hospitals, supermarkets and factories use computers, so do weather forecasters, airline pilots and train drivers.

◀ Using computers

We use computers to create documents, keep lists and records and search for information. A computer stores information, in the form of words, pictures, numbers and sounds, inside its memory.

▶ Hardware and software

A computer's hardware is the computer itself – the drives, the monitor, the keyboard and the printer. The software is the information, called data, inside the computer's memory as well as programs that you load onto a computer to give instructions.

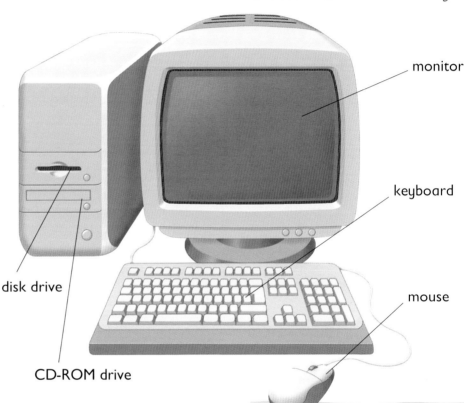

monitor

keyboard

mouse

disk drive

CD-ROM drive

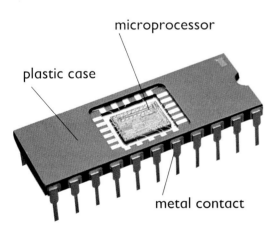

microprocessor

plastic case

metal contact

▲ Tiny chips

Microchips are tiny pieces of a hard material called silicon. We sometimes call them silicon chips. Each chip carries thousands of electrical paths called circuits. Microchips make up the 'brain' of your computer.

▼ Robot workers

In factories, computers control machines that carry out many jobs automatically. The robot that is spraying paint onto this car body is controlled by a computer.

Word scramble

Unscramble these words to find the names of four important parts of a computer:

a. somue
b. trepnir
c. romtion
d. kids rvide

answers
a. mouse b. printer
c. monitor d. disk drive

Conservation

Find out more:
Pollution ▶

Conservation involves looking after the plants and animals in our world, and protecting the wild places where they live. As human beings take up more and more space on the Earth, the places where plants and animals live are in danger. Some species have already disappeared completely.

dodo

◀ Disappearing animals

Some animals and plants have already died out – they have become extinct. The dodo was a flightless bird living on the island of Mauritius in the Indian Ocean. Its forest home was destroyed, and large numbers were hunted.

▼ Working for wildlife

Conservation work may involve planting trees, like the tree farm below, or helping to protect wildlife from being harmed.

▼ Tigers under threat

Tigers have already disappeared from much of Asia. Many have been hunted, or their homes destroyed. They may die out altogether in the next 100 years.

Wow!

The eggs of the extinct elephant bird from Madagsacar were big enough to hold eight litres of liquid – that's the same amount as in 24 soft drinks cans.

▼ Rare plants

In Great Britain, some types of plants such as the orchid are so rare that it is against the law to pick them in the wild.

orchid

▼ Gentle giants

Mountain gorillas are very rare in the mountain areas of Rwanda, in central Africa. Possibly fewer than 400 of these shy but powerful creatures still live there. Many have been killed or driven out by hunters.

Word box

illegal
not allowed by law

species
kind of plant or animal

Dance

All over the world people dance, usually to the sounds of music, as part of a ceremony or celebration, to express themselves, to entertain others – or simply to have fun. We know that people danced thousands of years ago. Paintings on cave walls show that prehistoric people used to dance before a hunting trip.

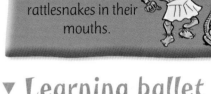

▲ Traditional dances

In African villages, dances are usually performed to celebrate important events such as births, weddings and good harvests. These Zulu villagers sing and clap as they dance in time to the beat of drums.

▼ Dragon dance

The Chinese celebrate each New Year's Day with a special parade. People dance through the streets wearing a large dragon costume. Chinese people believe that the dragon will keep away evil spirits during the year ahead.

▼ Learning ballet

Ballet dancers often start their training from a very early age. They have to practise hard to develop their strength and to learn all the movements perfectly.

▼ Carnival dancers

In Brazil, people dance in the street during carnival time.

Word box

carnival
a street celebration with music and dancing

prehistoric
a very long time ago

sacred
to do with religion

Deserts

Deserts are dry places where very little rain falls each year. Sometimes heavy rains in one year are followed by no rain at all for the next few years. Life for desert people can be very difficult. Many, such as the San people of Africa's Kalahari desert, are nomads. They move from place to place in search of water.

Wow!

The Atacama Desert in Chile, South America had no rain for 400 years. The rains finally arrived in 1971.

▶ Desert water

Oases lie near sources of water, such as springs or underground streams. Plants can grow here, so people often settle in these areas.

▲ Clever plants

Most deserts are near the Equator, the imaginary line that runs around the centre of the Earth. These deserts are hot and dry and few plants can survive. One type of desert plant, the cactus, stores water in its thick, fleshy stems.

▲ Polar deserts

Deserts are not always hot. The icy lands around the North and South Poles are known as cold deserts.

▶ Keeping cool

Animals in hot deserts try to avoid the extreme daytime heat by hiding beside rocks or underground. They come out in the cool night-time air to look for food.

Key
1 - kangaroo rat
2 - rattlesnake
3 - tarantula
4 - ringtail
5 - chuckwalla
6 - fennec fox
7 - long-nosed bat
8 - mule deer

Dinosaurs

Dinosaurs were reptiles that roamed the Earth millions of years ago. The giant ones were the largest creatures ever to have lived on land. **The smallest dinosaur,** *Compsognathus,* **was the same size as a chicken. These prehistoric creatures roamed the Earth for 160 million years until they died out suddenly, around 60 million years ago.**

Compsognathus

Wow!

Ultrasaurus, the heaviest dinosaur, weighed about 120 tonnes – that's 20 times heavier than a fully grown African elephant.

▶ Fierce hunters

Tyrannosaurus Rex was one of the fiercest, largest meat-eating dinosaurs. It was 12 metres long and hunted large, plant-eating dinosaurs such as *Iguanodon*.

▲ Flying reptiles

Pterodactyls were the largest of the flying dinosaurs. Even though they had enormous wing spans of up to 12 metres, they were very good fliers.

▼ Finding fossils

Everything we know about dinosaurs comes from fossils, the hard remains of animals found in rocks. People began to study dinosaurs after an English woman found a huge tooth buried in rock. Her husband realized that the tooth probably came from a giant reptile that looked like an iguana.

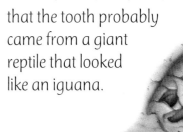

▲ Dinosaur defences

Stegosaurus was a plant-eating dinosaur that walked on all four legs. A row of bony plates along its back protected it from attack. These plates may have helped to cool the dinosaur's body too.

Word box

iguana
a kind of lizard

prehistoric
a very long time ago

The Earth is a huge, rocky ball spinning around in space. It is more than 4,600 million years old. Its surface is covered with large areas of land surrounded by sea. The layers of air around the Earth make up its atmosphere. In the atmosphere are the gases that all living things need to stay alive.

South America

▲ Earth from space

This view was taken from a spacecraft high up above the Earth's surface. You can clearly see the shape of the continent of South America, surrounded by dark-blue water. The wispy white areas are patches of swirling clouds.

▼ Moving Earth

About 220 million years ago, all the continents were joined as one super continent, called Pangea. Very slowly, this continent began to break up.

Pangea

200 million years ago, Pangea had split into two huge continents called Laurasia and Gondwanaland

even today the continents are still moving – North America is moving very slowly away from Europe

◀ Hot rocks and metals

The outer layer of the Earth is called the crust. It is about 32 kilometres thick below the land but only 8 kilometres thick below the oceans and seas. The very centre of the Earth lies about 6,400 kilometres below the surface – that's about the same distance as crossing North America from one side of the continent to the other.

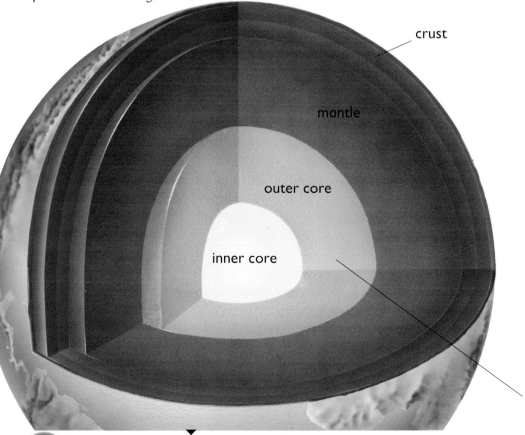

crust

mantle

outer core

inner core

in places the temperature is so hot that the rocks and metals have melted and become liquid

Earth features

Find out more:
Deserts ◄ Mountains ► Oceans and seas ►
Rocks and minerals ► Volcanoes ►

There are many wonderful sights on the surface of our amazing planet. They include thundering waterfalls, steep cliffs by the seashore and huge caves deep underground. Some of these features took millions of years to form.

▼ On the surface

Lots of different features cover the Earth's surface, such as snowy mountains, deep valleys, rocky deserts and enormous ice sheets.

▼ Natural disaster

An earthquake is a natural disaster. It can cause serious damage in just a few seconds. It is the violent shaking of the rocks inside the Earth.

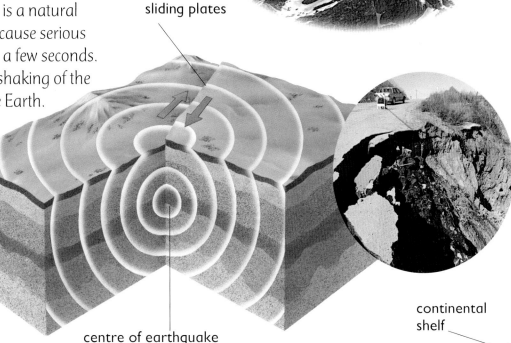

sliding plates

huge cracks can appear in the Earth's surface and can cause damage to buildings and roads.

centre of earthquake

continental shelf

material left by river currents

continental slope

▼ Deep down

Far below the surface of the oceans lies another landscape – on the floor of the ocean. Here there are mountains, wide plains and slopes and deep sea trenches.

ocean ridge

deep sea trench

Egyptians

About 5,000 years ago, the kingdom of ancient Egypt grew up in North Africa. At its centre lay the river Nile. This provided the Egyptians with water for themselves and their crops. Each year the river flooded, carrying fertile, black soil onto the land. Farmers were able to grow plenty of food.

▲ The river Nile

Travel by boat on the Nile was the most common way of getting around in ancient Egypt. The first boats were made of reeds from the papyrus plants that grew along the riverbank.

▼ Picture writing

The Egyptians used a kind of picture writing called hieroglyphics. Each picture stood for a different

word or sound. The pictures were painted onto walls.

▼ The pyramids

The Egyptians built spectacular tombs for their dead rulers, who were called pharaohs. The biggest tombs were the three huge pyramids at Giza. The Great Pyramid, which contains more than two million blocks of stone, took over 20 years to build.

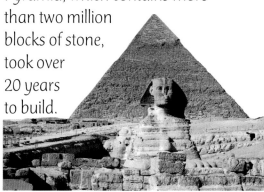

▶ Gods and goddesses

Horus

The Egyptians worshipped more than 1,000 different gods and goddesses. One of these, Horus, who protected the pharaoh, had a falcon's head.

◀ Buried treasure

The Egyptians believed that dead people went on to another life. They filled their dead rulers' tombs with things they thought they might need in the next life. These included jewels, food, even pets. This gold mask was found in the tomb of the boy-king Tutankhamun.

Word box

falcon
a fierce hunting bird

fertile
produces good crops

tomb
a special place where somebody is buried

Electricity

Electricity is one of our most useful kinds of energy. It lights up our streets and homes and powers our computers, televisions and washing machines. Even some trains are powered by electricity. Most of our electricity comes along cables from power stations to our homes.

◀ Giant spark

The lightning you see in a stormy sky is really an enormous spark of electricity. The heat from lightning is so powerful that it can set trees and houses alight.

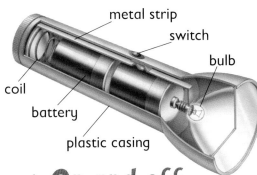

metal strip

switch

bulb

coil

battery

plastic casing

Word box

attract
to pull towards

cable
a thick wire that carries electricity

▼ Battery power

Machines such as torches and hand-held computer games are powered by batteries. Inside a battery are chemicals, which react with each other to produce electricity. Cars use huge batteries to start up their engine.

▲ On and off

When you switch on a torch, electricity flows from the battery to the bulb and lights it up. The electricity flows along a path called a circuit. When you switch the torch off, you break the circuit. The flow of electricity stops and the torch goes out.

▼ Sun power

Did you know you can make electricity from sunshine? The solar panels shown below turn light from the Sun into electricity. The electricity is used to pump water and to provide power for household equipment.

What is static electricity?

Comb your hair quickly for about 15 seconds on a dry day. Now hold the comb close to your head – your hair will stand on end. Comb your hair quickly again and hold the comb over some small pieces of paper. What happens? The combing action fills your comb with static electricity. Your hair, and the pieces of paper, are attracted by this static electricity.

Energy

Find out more:
Cars ◄ Electricity ◄ Energy sources ► Light at work ►
Oil and gas ► Sun ►

The engine inside a motor car needs energy to work. It gets this energy by burning a fuel such as petrol or diesel. Something that has energy is able to do work. Your body also needs energy – to run, skip, think and even to sleep. Your energy comes from the food you eat – it's your body's fuel.

▼ Heat and light

Energy from the Sun reaches the Earth as heat and light. Some of that energy is stored inside fuels such as coal, oil and gas.

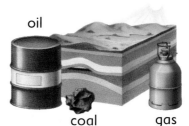

oil

coal   gas

Word box

active
busy, full of energy

coiled
wound up into rings or spirals

► How much energy?

A young, active person whose body is still growing needs lots of energy. So does an athlete, or a builder doing heavy work. Older people and office workers need less energy because they are not so active.

▼ Stored energy

What has a coiled spring to do with energy? The answer is that energy is stored inside the coiled spring, ready to do work. Some watches have a spring inside. When you wind up the watch you are storing energy inside the spring. As the spring unwinds, it turns the hands of the watch.

the spring is wound and energy is slowly released

the spring is hidden beneath this wheel

bread and cereals

fish and meat

▼ Energy foods

All the energy we get from food starts out as green plants. Humans eat plants (vegetables and fruit) and animals (meat and fish). The animals we eat have received their energy from eating green plants. Here are some of the foods we get our energy from.

cheese, butter and oil

fruit, vegetables and dairy products

Wow!

A 100-gram serving of peanut butter contains 2,600 times more energy than 100 grams of lettuce.

Energy sources

Most of the energy in our world comes from the Sun. Without it, the plants that provide us with food could not grow. Fuels such as coal and oil are made from the remains of plants and animals that lived along ago. These living things used the Sun's energy to grow.

▲ Harmful air

When we burn oil it produces harmful waste gases and dirt that enter the air. The air in many cities is filled with these waste gases from motor cars and factories.

▼ Nuclear energy

Some of our electricity comes from nuclear power stations. Instead of using the heat from burning oil or coal, a nuclear power station uses the heat energy released when atoms of nuclear fuel are split. The splitting process is carefully controlled in order to be safe.

▲ Water power

A hydroelectric power station uses the energy in water from a fast-flowing river or a dam to produce electricity. Flowing water is a source of energy that will never run out. We call it a renewable source – one that can be used again and again.

▼ Important fuel

Oil is one of the world's most important fuels. We take oil from deep under the sea or the ground, where it lies trapped between layers of rock. Oil drilling machinery is kept on special platforms out at sea, like the one shown here.

Word box

atom
a very tiny part of something

dam
a barrier specially built to hold back water

▶ Wind power

The energy in wind has been used for many thousands of years to turn the sails of windmills. We now use this wind energy to produce electricity. A large group of wind turbines is called a wind farm.

Europe

Europe is the smallest of the seven continents. It is a land of pine forests, grassy plains, snow-topped mountains and hot, sunny coastlines. The northern part of Europe has cold winters and warm summers while the countries around the Mediterranean Sea have hot, dry summers and mild winters.

▲ The far north

The far north of Europe is dotted with thousands of small islands and deep sea-filled valleys called fjords, like the one above. Places in the far north have long, cold winters where it stays dark for much of each day.

▲ Flat lands

Land beside the North Sea coast is extremely flat – some of it is even below sea level. Because of this, Belgium and the Netherlands are called the 'Low Countries'.

▲ Busy river

The Danube river crosses central Europe, from its source in Germany to its mouth on the shores of the Black Sea. Ships and barges carry agricultural products, steel and chemicals on the busy waters.

▼ Snowy mountains

The Alps stretch in a curve from southeast France across northern Italy, Switzerland and into Austria. In winter, thousands of tourists come to ski on the snowy slopes.

▲ Hot and dry

In the dry, sunny climate of southern Europe groves of olive trees and orange and lemon trees are a common sight. Vineyards produce grapes for the wine industry. Tourists spend holidays along the Mediterranean coast.

European people

Europe is a continent of many different peoples, cultures and languages. It is also very crowded, particularly the towns and cities of countries such as the Netherlands and Belgium. Since the time of the ancient Greeks, Europeans have probably changed the world more than any other group of people. They have taken their languages, inventions, religions, ideas, art and music to almost every corner of the world.

◄ Historic cities

Europe has many historic cities, with magnificent sights. In the 1400s and 1500s the Italian city of Florence was a meeting place for painters, musicians and writers.

▲ East and west

In 1990 East and West Germany were joined together again – Germany was divided at the end of World War II. Berlin, also once divided, became the capital of the new Germany. The city's Brandenburg Gate used to mark the boundary of the divided city.

► United countries

This is the flag of the European Union. Fifteen European countries belong to the European Union, an organization that involves countries working together closely on important matters such as money, jobs, industry and farming.

► Industry at work

Important industries in Europe include car manufacturing, food processing and chemicals and plastics. Many of the world's big car companies, for example Ford, have factories in several European countries.

Naming the country

Can you name these European countries?

a.

b.

c.

answers
a. Italy b. France
c. United Kingdom

Explorers

Christopher Columbus

In the past, explorers set off for unknown lands to look for riches, other people to trade with and places to settle. Some of the earliest explorers were Greek traders who explored the lands around the Mediterranean Sea. With the invention of stronger ships and better maps, many European explorers set sail to discover new lands in the 1400s. It was around this time that Christopher Columbus first reached America.

▲ Marco Polo

A young Italian called Marco Polo explored China and parts of Asia during the 1200s. He was a popular visitor at the court of the Chinese emperor, Kublai Khan.

▼ Heading west

Two Americans called Meriwether Lewis and William Clark set off in 1804 to explore the northwest United States. They travelled more than 12,000 kilometres during their two-year expedition.

Lewis and Clark travelled with the help of Native American guides

▼ Around the world

Ferdinand Magellan led the first sea voyage around the world. He set sail in 1519 but was killed towards the end of the journey. Only one of his ships completed the journey.

▼ Deep sea diver

In 1960, two men inside the diving vehicle *Trieste* descended more than 10 kilometres into the Marianas Trench, the deepest part of the Pacific Ocean.

▲ Antarctic disaster

Captain Robert Scott's second expedition to reach the South Pole ended in tragedy. When his team finally reached the South Pole on January 18, 1912, they found that a Norwegian team had arrived there one month earlier. Scott and his men died from hunger and cold on the way home.

Wow!

In 2000, British explorer David Hempleman-Adams attempted to fly over the Arctic Ocean to the North Pole in a hot-air balloon. He flew to within a few kilometres of the North Pole.

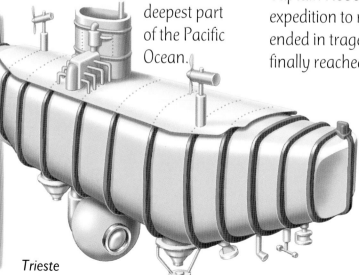

Trieste

Farming

Farmers across the world grow crops and rear animals to provide food for people to eat. In poorer countries, farmers usually work on small plots of land using simple tools and traditional methods. In countries such as the United States, farming is carried out on a large scale and huge machines do much of the work.

Wow!
A cotton-picking machine harvests the same amount of cotton as 80 people picking the cotton by hand.

► Plains of wheat

The Prairies, the wide, grassy plains of North America, are one of the world's largest wheat-producing areas. Large herds of cattle are reared here, too.

▲ Giant machines

In richer countries, giant machines called combine harvesters gather in the ripe crops at harvest time. In poorer countries the harvest is cut by hand.

▼ Ploughing land

This Asian farmer is ploughing land with a plough pulled by oxen. He will use this land to grow crops such as rice, millet and wheat.

▲ Sheep-rearing

Farming differs from place to place, depending on the soil, climate and the shape of the land. The mild, wet climate of New Zealand is well suited to rearing sheep, because there is plenty of good grazing land. More sheep than people live in New Zealand!

▼ Planting seeds

These Chinese farmers are planting rice seedlings by hand. Because there are so many people to feed in China, farmers have to use as much land as possible to grow food. Terraces are cut into hillsides to make them suitable for growing crops.

Word box

millet
a plant crop producing tiny seeds that are crushed to make flour

terrace
a flat, step-like area cut out of a piece of land

Fish

Fish can live anywhere there is water – icy oceans, freshwater lakes, fast-flowing rivers and tropical seas. Some fish, such as the walking catfish, can even survive for a few days on land. Fish come in many different sizes, from the tiny pygmy goby, which is smaller than your fingernail, to the 12-metre-long whale shark.

Word box

freshwater
non-salty water in lakes and rivers

tropical
with warm water in hot parts of the world

▶ Fishy parts

A fish has special parts called gills to let it breathe underwater. It uses its gills to take in oxygen from the water. Fish use their fins to help them swim.

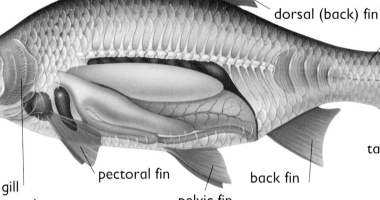

dorsal (back) fin | scales

tail fin

pectoral fin

back fin

gill openings

pelvic fin

◀ Surface to floor

More than 13,000 kinds of fish live in the oceans and seas. Most swim at the surface, like the tuna (1) and the blue marlin (2). Others, such as the oar fish (3) and the lantern fish (4), live deeper down. A few, such as the tripod fish (5) and the gulper eel (6), live close to the ocean floor.

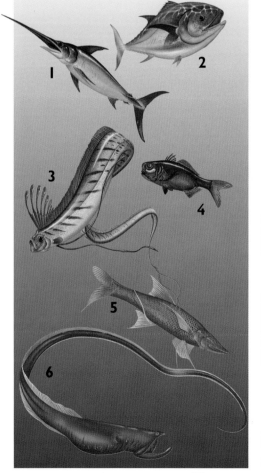

▼ In freshwater

Freshwater fish such as perch and trout live in rivers, streams and lakes. Some fish live in streams that flow deep under the ground. Most freshwater fish cannot survive in the salty oceans and seas.

perch

Word scramble

Unscramble these words to find the names of four saltwater fish.

a. grenhir
b. dakcodh
c. utan
d. tiblahu

answers
a. herring b. haddock c. tuna d. halibut

▲ Fishy killers

Many sharks are fierce hunters. They have strong teeth and jaws and can attack fish and dolphins with great speed. This blue shark can grow up to 3.8 metres in length.

Flowers

Flowers are the brightly coloured, sweet-smelling parts of plants such as roses, tulips, orchids and lilies. Yet not all flowers are colourful and fragrant. Some plants, such as grasses, produce small flowers with no smell at all. All flowers produce seeds that are needed for new flowering plants.

◄ Busy bees

This bee is collecting pollen in tiny 'baskets' on its back legs. It will carry the pollen to another flower.

Word box

bloom
to produce flowers

fragrant
sweet-smelling

sprout
to begin to grow

► Flowery parts

Each flower has male parts called stamens and female parts called carpels. Stamens produce tiny grains of pollen. Usually, pollen from one flower has to reach the female parts of another flower before seeds can start to grow.

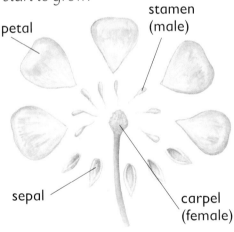

petal

stamen (male)

sepal

carpel (female)

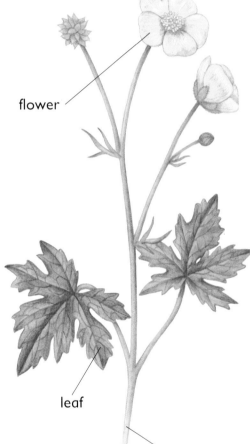

flower

leaf

stem

roots

▼ Flower gardens

You can see displays of flowers in parks and gardens everywhere. People have enjoyed growing and arranging flowers since the time of the ancient Egyptians.

▼ In the desert

Desert flowers usually bloom after a burst of rain. The seeds lie in the ground when it is dry, and then start to sprout as soon as the rain arrives.

A wildflower garden

It's really easy to grow flowers. Why don't you try planting your own wildflower garden in a spare patch of land (don't forget to ask an adult first)? Your wildflower garden will attract insects such as butterflies and bees. You could dry and press the flowers and use them to decorate your own stationery.

Flying machines

The first flying machine, or aircraft, to carry people through the air was a hot-air balloon. It was built by the French Montgolfier brothers, and in 1783 it flew for about eight kilometres. Two hundred years later, people could fly at supersonic speeds (faster than the speed of sound) in specially designed jet aircraft.

◀ Hot air

Two passengers travelled in the Montgolfier balloon in the skies above Paris, the capital of France. The linen balloon was filled with air heated by burning straw and wool.

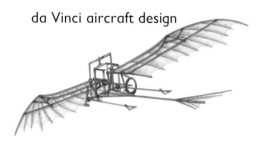

da Vinci aircraft design

▲ Early plane

An Italian artist and inventor called Leonardo da Vinci (1452–1519) produced one of the first aircraft designs, in the 1500s. The aircraft's wings flapped like a bird's wings.

▶ War planes

During World War I, the design of aircraft improved. By the end of the war, planes could fly more quickly and most were made from metal, not wood.

▼ Airships

Like balloons, airships are filled with gas, but they also have engines and steering equipment. Travel by airship was popular until 1937, when the *Hindenburg*, a huge airship filled with hydrogen gas, exploded near New York, USA. Thirty-six people on board were killed.

the *Hindenburg*

flying boat

▲ Flying boats

In the 1920s and 1930s a few people travelled abroad in large aircraft that landed on water. These seaplanes were called flying boats. They made regular flights across the Atlantic Ocean between Europe and North America.

▶ The first flight

Two American brothers, Orville and Wilbur Wright, were the first people to make a powered, heavier-than-air aircraft fly. In 1903 their *Flyer* aeroplane flew over Kitty Hawk in California, USA, for 12 seconds.

Flying today

Today, the biggest passenger airliners are known as wide-bodied jets. Wide-bodied aircraft such as the latest 747s can carry over 600 passengers for very long distances without stopping to refuel. Small planes that carry just a few passengers are known as light aircraft. We use them to deliver mail, to carry small groups of passengers on short journeys and to make special flights such as the delivery of emergency supplies. Most pilots learn to fly in light aircraft.

▼ Jumbo jets

This modern passenger plane is a Boeing 747. These planes are nicknamed 'jumbo jets' because of their enormous size.

a helicopter has long, spinning blades, called a rotor, instead of wings

the smaller rotor on the tail stops the helicopter from spinning round in the opposite direction from the rotor on top

Wow!

In 1999 *Breitling Orbiter* became the first hot-air balloon to fly non-stop around the world. The journey took 21 days.

▼ Power and speed

These powerful jet fighters can perform twists and turns in the air at the same time as each other. This is called flying in formation.

▲ Helicopters

Helicopters carry people or supplies to places that are difficult to reach.

▼ Crop-sprayer

This light aircraft is used for spraying chemicals over a field of crops. The chemicals kill harmful insects and other pests.

Word box

pests
small animals that can cause damage to crops

spinning
turning around very fast

Food

Find out more:
Energy ◀ Farming ◀ Human body ▶ Plants ▶
Plants around the world ▶

All human beings need food to stay alive.
Food gives us the energy to work and play. It also helps our bodies grow and stay healthy. Most people enjoy eating food, too. A meal is a time when we sit down with family or friends. Sometimes people eat special foods to celebrate an event, such as a religious festival or a birthday.

▼ Fast food

Hamburgers, hot dogs and French fries are known as fast food. This kind of food can contain a lot of fats. Too many fats can make you unhealthy.

▼ Growing food

Huge areas of wheat and other crops grow in Canada and the USA. Some of this food is sold to countries that do not grow enough food of their own.

▶ Different milk

In Great Britain and North America, most of the milk that people drink is from cows. In other parts of the world, milk comes from sheep, goats – even camels.

◀ After the harvest

We buy fruits and vegetables soon after they have been harvested (picked). Fresh foods like these can be bought at markets and supermarkets. Other foods, such as wheat, are sent to factories to be made into bread and pasta.

▼ Not enough food

A famine occurs when there is not enough food. People can starve and die. A lack of rain is the usual cause of a famine.

no rain means that plants die

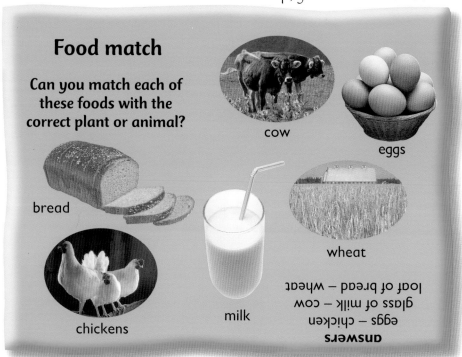

Food match

Can you match each of these foods with the correct plant or animal?

bread

cow

eggs

wheat

chickens

milk

answers
eggs – chicken
glass of milk – cow
loaf of bread – wheat

Forests

Find out more:
Air ◄   Conservation ◄   Plants ►   Plants around the world ►
Rainforests ►   Trees ►

Forests cover about one-fifth of the Earth's land. Every forest is filled with millions of living things, from tiny creatures that bury themselves under the leaves on the forest floor to the birds that nest high up in the branches.

the red squirrel makes its home in forest branches

Wow!

Scientists found 10,500 different kinds of living thing in a deciduous forest in Switzerland.

▼ Forest animals

Many animals find food and shelter in the forest. Small creatures such as squirrels and mice feed on leaves, fruits and seeds. They are eaten by larger animals such as stoats, weasels and wild cats.

wild cat

deer

stoat

tortoise

shrew

mouse   toad   snail   snake

◄ Cold forests

In cool parts of the world, and in mountain areas, grow conifers — trees such as pines, firs and spruces. These trees are evergreens — they keep their leaves all year round.

▼ Changing colour

In places with warm summers and cool winters, many forests are deciduous. This means their trees have leaves that change colour and fall off.

▼ Oxygen-givers

All forests have an important job to do. Their trees take in carbon dioxide gas from the air and give off oxygen, the gas that all animals need to stay alive.

Fossils

A fossil is the remains of a plant or animal that lived a very long time ago. It can be the shell, the skeleton or just the outline shape of a dead animal. It can also be the marks left by an animal as it moved across the land. By studying fossils, scientists have learned much about the plants and animals that lived on the Earth thousands and millions of years ago.

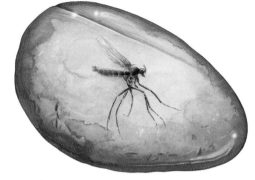

▲ Trapped!

The whole body of this insect has turned into a fossil. Millions of years ago, it was trapped inside the sticky substance that oozed from pine trees. The sticky stuff hardened to form amber, which we make into jewellery and ornaments.

▼ Making fossils

Fossils are usually found inside rocks that were once covered by seawater.

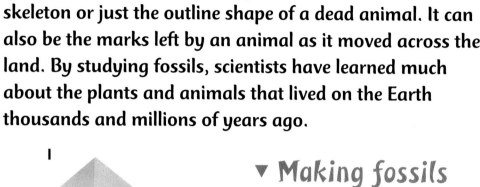

1. when a sea creature died, its body fell to the sea-bed

2. it was then covered by mud and sand

3. seawater dissolved the bones, and the mud and sand slowly turned into rock

4. the hollow shape of the animal was left in the rock

Solve the riddle

Solve this riddle to find a five-letter word.
My first is in RAIN but not in REIGN.
My second is in MOLE but not in POLES.
My third is in ABLE but not in TALE.
My fourth is in TEA but not in TAR.
My last is in ROSE but not in TOES.

answer: AMBER

► Discovered!

In far northern parts of the world, scientists have found the bodies of woolly mammoths which lived thousands of years ago. The skin, hair and body parts of the mammoths, such as those shown here, had been preserved in the frozen ground.

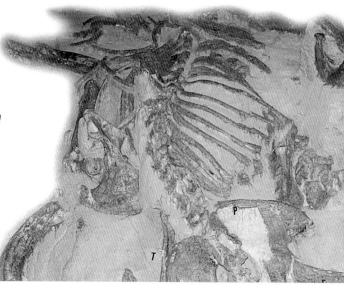

Grasslands

Africa ◄ Farming ◄

Wide, flat areas of grassland are found in most of the world's continents. Grasslands have different names in different places of the world. The hot, dry grasslands of East Africa are savannahs, while those in South America are known as pampas. The grassy plains in central Asia are called steppes.

◄ From place to place

Mongolian nomads live on the grassland steppes of central Asia, where they raise herds of goats, cattle and yaks. These nomads live in tents called yurts, which are traditionally covered with felt.

Word box

felt
cloth made from pieces of wool that are pressed together

hide
the skin of an animal

nomad
someone who moves from place to place in search of grazing land

▼ The prairies

The grasslands of North America are called prairies. The soil here is fertile, and most of the grasslands have been ploughed up and turned into farmland for growing crops and rearing beef cattle.

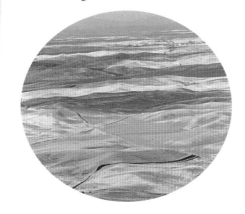

Animal antics

Which of these animals lives on the grasslands of Africa?

a. lion
b. crocodile
c. gorilla
d. ostrich

answers
a. lion d. ostrich

▲ Buffaloes

Millions of American bison, or buffalo, used to graze on the North American Prairies. Between 1850 and 1890, European settlers killed around 20 million of them, for their meat and hides. By 1889, only 551 bison were left alive.

► In Africa

Large herds of zebra, antelope, wildebeest and other grazing animals wander across the savannah of East Africa. The animals are always on the look-out for danger from hunters such as lions and leopards.

a b c d e f **g** h i j k l m n o p q r s t u v w x y z 51

Greeks

The people of ancient Greece had many important ideas about science, buildings, art, drama, poetry, athletics and government. Today we still feel the influence of these clever people, who lived more than 2,000 years ago. One of the most famous ideas handed down from that time is the Olympic Games. In ancient Greece, this sporting contest was held every four years to honour the ruler of the gods, Zeus.

Ares
Athene
Aphrodite

▶ Greek gods

The Greeks worshipped gods and goddesses, who they believed looked after them in daily life. Zeus was ruler of all the gods. Shown here are Aphrodite, goddess of love, Athene, goddess of wisdom and Ares, god of war.

▶ Painted pots

Greek pottery was usually painted with scenes from daily life, or popular myths about gods and goddesses.

▼ Temples and theatres

The Greeks built magnificent temples, such as the Parthenon on the hilltop overlooking the city of Athens. The temple was dedicated to Athene, the goddess of wisdom. The Greeks also built huge, open-air theatres with seating for thousands of spectators.

▼ Greek maths

The Greeks were clever scientists and mathematicians. One famous mathematician, called Euclid, wrote several books on geometry. His ideas about this subject are still taught in schools today.

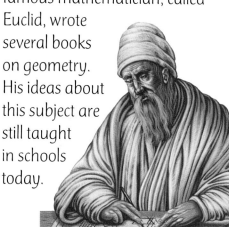

Wow!

In ancient Greece the Olympic Games were for male athletes only – and only male spectators were allowed to watch.

Homes

Your home protects you from the heat and the cold, and from rain and snow. It is the place where you usually sleep, eat your meals and relax with family and friends. Around the world people build many different styles of home to suit their way of life, the local climate and the building materials that are available.

▲ Houses in rows

A row of homes joined together like this is typical of many European cities and towns. These houses are built from baked clay bricks.

▲ Up on stilts

These homes in southeast Asia are built on stilts to protect the occupants from swampy ground around their village. The land sometimes floods, so the stilts keep the houses above the water level.

▼ A house of reeds

This is the home of a family of Marsh Arabs, who live by the river Tigris in Iraq. For thousands of years people here have built homes from reeds cut from the riverbank.

▲ Keeping cool

These houses in Africa are made from wood and thick straw. The thick roofs help to keep the inside of the house cool when temperatures outside are very hot.

▲ A tented home

Bedouins live in large tents in the hot deserts of the Middle East and North Africa. Bedouins raise herds of sheep, goats and camels. They move their tents from place to place in search of water and fresh grazing for their animals. ▼

▶ Tall homes

A multi-storey block of apartments is one way of saving space in a crowded city centre. Large numbers of families can make their home inside a single building.

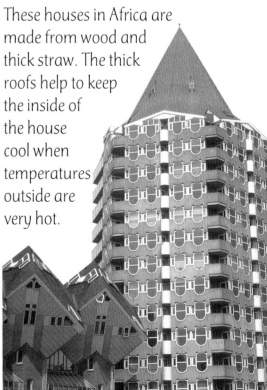

Human body

Find out more:
Babies ◄ Human skeleton ► Mammals and their babies ►

Your body is like a busy, complicated machine.
Every machine needs fuel and regular use, and it's the same for your body. Your body has many different parts that work together to keep you alive. The brain is your body's control centre and it tells your body what to do. How you breathe, move, think and feel are controlled by your brain.

▼ Pumping blood

blood with oxygen is taken to the body

Your heart beats about 100,000 times a day to pump blood around your body. Fresh blood travels from your heart to every part of your body. Stale blood goes back to your heart and then to your lungs to collect supplies of oxygen.

stale blood enters the heart

fresh blood is pumped around your body

► From head to toe

Skin covers your body from the top of your head to the soles of your feet. Your skin is tough and stretchy – and it's waterproof, too. It keeps out harmful germs and stops you from getting too hot or too cold.

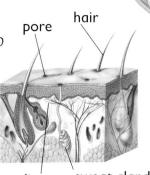

pore   hair

nerve endings   sweat gland

◄ Your senses

You have five senses that tell you what is happening around you. They let you see, hear, smell, touch and taste. Your brain sends messages to your sense organs. These are your eyes, ears, nose, skin and mouth.

messages from your brain travel to every part of your body

you use your lungs to breathe

your heart pumps blood around your body

your kidneys get rid of waste material from your blood

broken-down pieces of food pass from your intestines into your blood

Count your heartbeat

Place two fingers on the inside of your wrist. If you press gently you will feel a throbbing. This is your pulse. Each throb is one heartbeat, as your heart pumps blood around your body. How many times does your heart beat in one minute?

Human skeleton

Without a skeleton you would be like a floppy bean bag. Your skeleton holds you together and gives your body its shape. It protects soft parts such as your heart and lungs. Joined to the bones of your skeleton are muscles. You use muscles to move every part of your body. There are even muscles in your face which help you to smile or frown.

▶ Broken bones

If you break a bone in your arm or leg it is usually set in a plaster cast. Sometimes metal plates like this one are used to help bones mend.

▶ On the move

Muscles pull on your bones to make them move. You use muscles to walk, run, jump – even to breathe. Your body has more than 650 muscles.

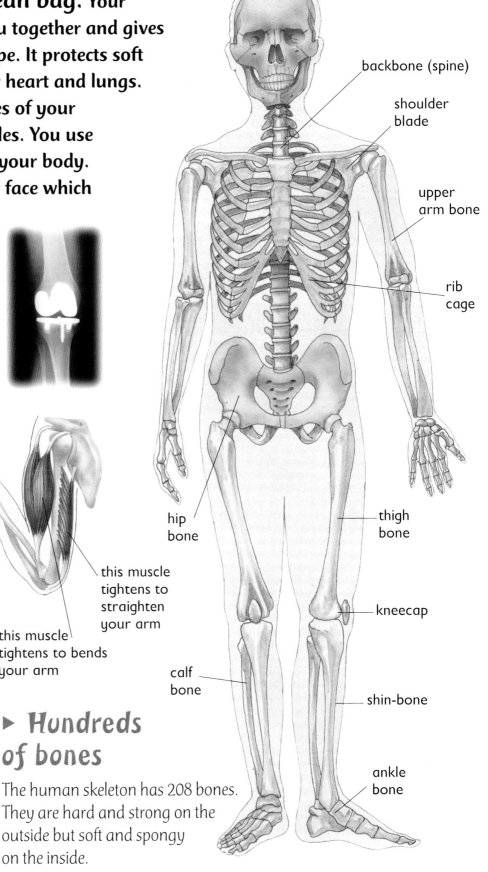

skull

backbone (spine)

shoulder blade

upper arm bone

rib cage

hip bone

this muscle tightens to straighten your arm

this muscle tightens to bends your arm

calf bone

thigh bone

kneecap

shin-bone

ankle bone

Word scramble

Unscramble these words to find the names of four important body parts:

a. thare
b. kleonest
c. sculem
d. inbar

answers: a. heart **b.** skeleton **c.** muscle **d.** brain

▶ Hundreds of bones

The human skeleton has 208 bones. They are hard and strong on the outside but soft and spongy on the inside.

Insects

Butterflies and bees, moths and mosquitoes, cockroaches and crickets are all types of insect. Altogether there are almost one million different kinds of insect – and scientists think there are millions more that have not yet been named. Most insects are very small creatures, less than one centimetre long. There are some large ones, however, such as the giant Hercules moth from Australia, whose open wings measure 30 centimetres from tip to tip.

leg

abdomen

thorax

antenna

stag beetle

head

Word box

hatch
to come out of an egg

pupa
protective covering around
a developing butterfly

thorax
the part of an insect that bears
its legs and wings

◄ Body parts

All insects have six legs arranged in pairs. An insect's body is divided into three main parts: the head, the thorax and the abdomen. Most insects have wings and antennae, too.

▼ All colours

Some insects, such as dragon flies, are very colourful but others are a dull brown or black colour. Some look like leaves, sticks or tree bark to hide themselves from enemies. Others have bold spots or stripes to scare enemies away.

dragon fly

► Butterfly life

All insects begin life as an egg. Caterpillars hatch from the eggs of a butterfly. A young caterpillar looks nothing like the adult butterfly. When a caterpillar stops growing, it turns into a pupa. Finally, an adult butterfly crawls out of the pupa.

1. the female butterfly lays her eggs and dies

5. the butterfly is ready to fly after about an hour

4. finally the adult butterfly pushes its way out of the pupa

1

2

3

4

5

2. the caterpillar hatches from the egg. It spends most of its time eating

3. when the caterpillar is fully grown, it is ready to turn into a pupa. A hard shell begins to form around it, protecting the butterfly developing inside

Insects at work

Find out more:
Animal kingdom ◄ Flowers ◄ Insects ◄
Light at work ►

Most insects have a very busy life. They have to build a home, look for a partner, hunt and collect food, fight enemies, lay eggs and look after their young. Some insects bite, spread disease and damage crops. However, insects are very important for life because they pollinate plants which form food for humans and animals.

bees carry pollen grains from plant to plant

▼ Huge nests

Termites live in big family groups called colonies. Some build tall nests that are home to thousands of termites. All the termites in a colony are the children of one female termite, the queen.

'chimney' can be 6 metres tall

wall made of earth

► Hungry insects

Locusts are a kind of grasshopper. They can travel long distances in huge crowds called swarms. One swarm may contain millions and millions of locusts. They swoop down to eat crops and other plants, destroying huge areas of plant life in a very short time.

locust

▼ Insect lights

Some insects even use special effects to help them find a mate. This firefly is able to flash a yellowish light on and off to attract other flies.

Word scramble

Unscramble these words to find the names of four insects:

a. AGRIWE
b. EBLETE
c. BLIYDRAD
d. GRANDLYOF

answers
a. earwig b. beetle c. ladybird d. dragonfly

► Going underground

These tall termite nests continue for some distance underground. Inside is a maze of chambers (rooms) where young are looked after by 'worker' termites and food is stored. Air passages keep the nest cool.

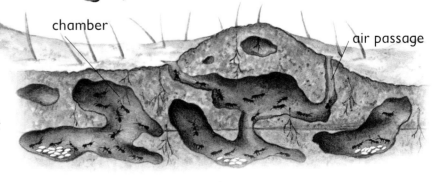

chamber

air passage

Jobs

Teacher, truck driver, dentist, sales assistant, builder and banker are kinds of job. A job is the work you do to earn money. Some people do outdoor jobs working on the land or at sea. Other jobs involve making things in factories and workshops, such as cars and computers. Some jobs provide help and information for others, for example in shops, hospitals, offices and banks.

Word box

assemble
to put together

natural resource
something useful from the land or the sea

▲ Helping others

Jobs in offices, banks, hotels and shops are called service jobs. These jobs involve organizing and helping instead of working with natural resources or making goods.

► Factory work

This man assembles computers in a giant factory, where he works with the help of complicated machines. Computers control some of these machines. Thousands of other workers have jobs in the same factory.

◄ From the sea

Once fish are caught from the sea in huge nets, people on board the fishing boat set to work sorting and cleaning the catch. The fish are then packed in ice to keep them fresh, and brought ashore for sale.

▼ By hand

This potter is working with his hands. He uses machines as well in his job, such as a special oven called a kiln to bake the pots hard.

Job search

The names of five jobs are hidden in this grid. Can you find them?

C	R	O	L	I	T	D	V
H	S	D	A	R	M	O	E
E	K	A	R	T	I	S	T
F	Z	G	I	O	N	H	R
P	L	A	W	Y	E	R	U
U	W	S	A	L	R	E	N

answers: vet lawyer miner chef artist

◄ Dangerous jobs

Fire-fighting can be a dangerous job. Fire-fighters have to be fit and strong and ready to risk their lives for other people. They also have to know about preventing fires, rescuing people and giving first aid in an emergency.

Kings

Kings have ruled over people and kingdoms for hundreds of years. Once, most kings had great power over their kingdoms. The majority of today's kings have much less control, and many have handed over their powers to a parliament elected by the people. There are still some powerful kings in Asia and Africa.

Wow!

Louis XIV's palace at Versailles, outside Paris, is almost half a kilometre long and has around 1,300 rooms.

▲ King Solomon

Solomon ruled over Israel about 1,000 years before the birth of Jesus Christ. He was a wise king and also a great builder. He ordered the building of the Temple in the city of Jerusalem.

▼ Beheaded!

Throughout history, people have sometimes turned against their king and tried to get rid of him. Charles I was king of England and Scotland in the 1600s. Although he lost a civil war in Britain, Charles still refused to give up his powers. He was finally beheaded in London on January 31, 1649.

▼ Sun King

Louis XIV (Louis the Fourteenth) of France (1638–1715) was a very extravagant king. He was nicknamed the 'Sun King' because he chose the Sun as his royal symbol. He ruled France for more than 70 years, fought several wars and also encouraged writers and artists.

the royal symbol of Louis XIV

▼ Tudor king

Henry VIII (the Eighth) was king of England from 1509 to 1547. He was the second Tudor king, and is best known for marrying six times during his reign, so desperate was he for a son. Jane Seymour, Henry's third wife, gave birth to a boy in 1537.

Light

Find out more:
Colour ◄ Energy ◄ Light at work ► Stars ► Sun ►

You need light to be able to see things. Light bounces off an object and travels into your eyes, letting you see the object. Light rays travel in straight lines. Light always travels like this until it meets an object, then it changes direction. But light can pass right through some materials, such as glass and water.

fibre optic cable

Word box

light year
the distance light can travel in one year

optical
relating to vision

◄ Starlight

Stars are so far away from the Earth that their light takes millions and millions of years to reach us. We describe the distance that starlight travels in light-years — one light-year is the distance that light can travel in one year. Our nearest stars are more than four light-years away, which is 40 million million kilometres!

▼ Bending light

When light travels through water, it bends and changes direction. We call this bending refraction. This is why a straw in a glass sometimes looks as if it's bending .

▼ Magic mirrors

When you look in a mirror you see your reflection. How? The mirror reflects the light from your face back into your eyes. The mirror's shiny surface is a good reflector.

▲ Light signals

Light helps you to make a telephone call. Light carries sound signals from your telephone to the phone of the person you are calling. The light travels along very thin threads of glass called optical fibres. Each fibre is only one millimetre wide.

Bend the straw

Why don't you try this experiment. Fill a glass halfway up and stand it on a table. Put a drinking straw in the glass so it leans against the side. The straw looks bent because light rays hitting the water changed direction.

Light at work

Colour ◄ Energy ◄ Light ◄ Insects at work ◄
Stars ►

Light can come from the Sun, from a candle, a torch, an electric lamp – even a tiny firefly. All these are sources of light. Without the light from the Sun there would be no life on Earth.

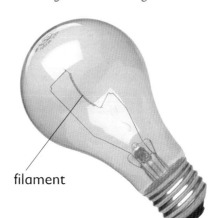

► Bright city lights

Advertising signs in city centres are often lit up with brightly coloured lights. These lights are called neon lights. They have a glass tube filled with a mixture of gases. Different gases glow different colours when electricity flows through the tube.

► Lighting the way

Before electric lights were invented, people used candles and oil lamps. In 1815 the Davy lamp was invented. This lit the way for miners underground, and gave protection from dangerous gases.

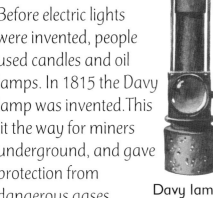

Davy lamp

filament

▲ Light bulbs

The coil of wire inside a light bulb is the filament. When electricity passes through the filament it heats up and glows white, giving off light.

▼ Glow in the dark

Some animals produce light of their own. The light from this glow worm acts as a signal to other glow worms that it is looking for a mate.

▼ Light as energy

Light is a kind of radiation which is really energy on the move. It is a type of radiation, known as electromagnetic. Microwaves are another type of electromagnetic radiation. These waves can be used to cook food.

microwave oven

Word box

filament
the thin wire inside a light bulb

radiation
energy that travels in waves

a b c d e f g h i j k **l** m n o p q r s t u v w x y z

61

Machines

All machines do work for us. Door handles, can openers and wheelbarrows are simple kinds of machine. Computers, printing presses and motor cars are large complicated machines. All these machines help us each day by letting us do different jobs more quickly and easily.

▼ Heavy loads

We use a wheelbarrow to move a load that is too heavy to lift by hand. It is really a simple machine called a lever. Levers help you to lift heavy weights without using a lot of effort. You move one end of a lever in order to lift a heavy load at the other end.

▶ In the home

Everyday machines such as vacuum cleaners, electric kettles, food processors and dishwashers help us to clean, cook and wash up more quickly.

vacuum cleaner

▶ Cranes

You can see cranes on building sites, in factories and in docks. We use cranes to lift and move heavy loads. A crane is a type of pulley, which is a simple machine made up of a wheel with a rope over it. You pull on one end of the rope to lift a heavy load attached to the other end.

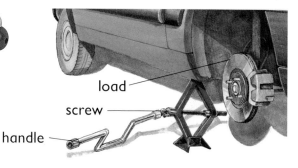

load

screw

handle

▼ Jet power

A jet engine is a very powerful machine. Large passenger aircraft have three or four jet engines. A stream of gases shoots out of the back of the engine and pushes the aircraft forwards through the air.

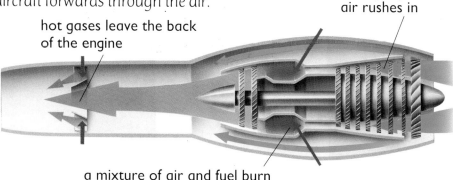

hot gases leave the back of the engine

air rushes in

a mixture of air and fuel burn

▲ Simple jack

A jack is made up of two kinds of simple machine: a lever and a screw. By moving the jack's handle, or lever, you turn the screw and lift up a heavy load such as a car. We use a jack when taking off an old car tyre or putting on a new one.

Machines in history

the *Gutenberg* Press

▲ Printing machine

This printing press was made in Germany about 550 years ago. The printer used it to make many copies of the same page of a book.

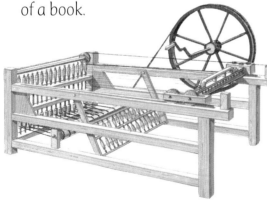

▲ Spinning jenny

This machine is called a spinning jenny. It is a kind of spinning wheel that spins lots of cotton threads at the same time. Before this machine was invented in 1764, each spinning wheel could only spin one thread at a time. In the cotton factories, spinning jennies allowed the spinners to produce enough cotton thread to keep the cotton weavers busy at work.

From the 1700s onwards, people started to use machines more and more to do their work. The first steam engine was made to pump water out of a tin mine in Cornwall, England. Later, steam engines were used to provide the power for hundreds of different machines, from weaving looms and spinning wheels to cars and ships.

the *Rocket* was a huge success, and proved that steam engines were of great use on railways

▲ Steam engine

The *Rocket* was the first modern steam engine. It was built by George and Robert Stephenson in 1829. It reached a top speed of 56 kilometres per hour.

▼ Motor cars

The motor car is one of the world's most popular machines. One of the first proper motor cars was this three-wheeled vehicle. It was built in 1886 by a German named Karl Benz. Its engine was powered by gas.

Wow!

The ancient Egyptians used a giant screw inside a cylinder-shaped container to take water from the river Nile. The machine was invented by a Greek mathematician called Archimedes.

Motorwagen, built by Karl Benz

Mammals

Find out more:
Animal kingdom ◀ Babies ◀ Mammals and their babies ▶

Bats and bears, monkeys and moles, wallabies and whales – all these animals are mammals.
Human beings are mammals, so are many of the animals we see around us – our pet cats and dogs, and farm animals such as sheep, cows and goats. Altogether there are about 4,500 different kinds of mammal.

dolphin

▼ The smallest

One of the smallest mammals is a bat. It is called Kitti's hog-nosed bat and is less than 2 centimetres long – about the same size as a bumble bee.

◀ Keeping warm

Whales, dolphins and porpoises are mammals that live in the water. Unlike most mammals, they do not have fur or hair. Instead, they have a layer of fat under the skin to keep their bodies warm.

▲ Odd mammals

The giant anteater of South America is a very strange-looking mammal. It eats only ants or termites, and its sharp claws are ideal for breaking into insect nests. The anteater's tongue extends to a length of 60 centimetres!

◀ Brainy!

Mammals have better developed brains than any other animal group. The most intelligent mammals, after humans, are monkeys and apes. Some chimpanzees use sticks as tools to catch termites!

▼ Comparing size

There are about 4,500 different types of mammal. The biggest, the blue whale, is shown to scale here with some other mammals. Even the biggest land mammal, the elephant, looks tiny next to the blue whale.

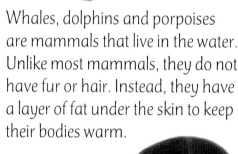

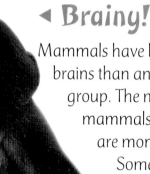

blue whale
33.5 metres long

giraffe 5.5 metres tall

human
1.7 metres tall

brown bear
2.4 metres tall

African elephant
3.3 metres tall

64 a b c d e f g h i j k l **m** n o p q r s t u v w x y z

Mammals and their babies

Find out more:
Animal kingdom ◄
Babies ◄ Mammals ◄

Mammals are the only animals that feed their young on milk. Many young mammals are born with hair or fur and they are cared for by their parents afterwards. A chimpanzee baby, for example, stays with its mother until it is about six years old.

▼ Living in a pouch

Kangaroos and koalas belong to a group of mammals called marsupials. They give birth to tiny, undeveloped babies. The babies crawl to a pouch on their mother's stomach. They stay there for about eight months, drinking their mother's milk until they are fully developed.

pouch entrance

1. newborn kangaroo crawls to its mother's pouch

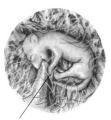

2. in the pouch, the baby drinks its mother's milk

duck-billed platypus

▲ Laying eggs

A few mammals lay eggs from which their young hatch. These mammals live in Australia and New Guinea. The duck-billed platypus is one of them. Its baby licks milk off its mother's belly.

the young kangaroo (joey) stays in the pouch until quite large, and covered in fur

▲ Biggest baby

The biggest mammal of all, the blue whale, also gives birth to the biggest baby. When it is born, the blue whale calf is already six to eight metres long. Its mother's milk is rich, which helps the baby to grow quickly.

▼ Caring for young

Most mammals care for their young for some time after they are born. Many young, like these cheetah cubs, rely on their mother for food and protection. They also learn how to hunt and look after themselves in the wild.

Word box

pouch
a pocket of skin

undeveloped
not fully-grown

Maps

We use some maps to find our way from place to place. Maps also give us information about an area of land – a map can tell you where hills and rivers are, where roads and railways run, which countries make up a continent or where to find a certain street in a big city.

▲ Maps for walkers

Hill-walkers use maps that show the physical features of the land, such as hills, valleys, rivers and lakes. Some physical maps also show the route of public footpaths, cycle tracks and nature trails.

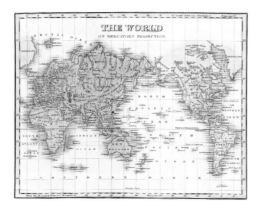

▲ A map for sailors

This world map shows how Gerardus Mercator, who came from Flanders (modern Belgium), thought the world looked. It was published in 1569. The map helped sailors find their way more easily.

▼ Matching maps

Here are two maps of Africa. The one on the right is a political map, it shows the different country boundaries. The one shown below is a physical map, it shows the natural features of the land, such as deserts, mountains and rivers.

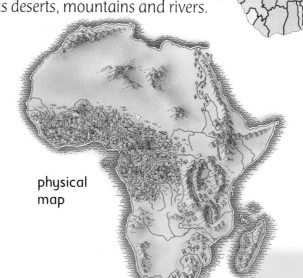

physical map

▼ Which direction?

Walkers, climbers, sailors and pilots need to know which direction they are travelling in before they can use a map properly. They find out with the help of a magnetic compass. It has a small needle that always points in the direction of north.

Wow!

One of the world's first maps was carved onto a clay tablet in the ancient city of Babylon 4,500 years ago.

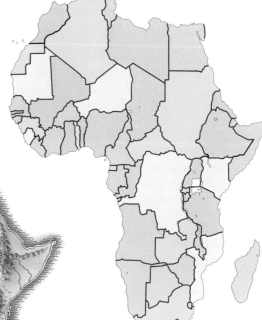

political map

Word box

boundary
a line that marks out an area, such as a country or a state

magnetic
points to North at one end and South at the other

tablet
a flat piece of a material such as wood or stone

Materials

Find out more:
Machines in history ◄ Rocks and minerals ►
Spacecraft ►

Wool, paper, copper, steel, concrete and plastic – all of these are materials. We use materials to make things. We choose the right material for the right thing. For example, a ball is not made out of glass or paper because they are not suitable materials. Instead we choose a material, such as rubber, because it is stretchy and bouncy.

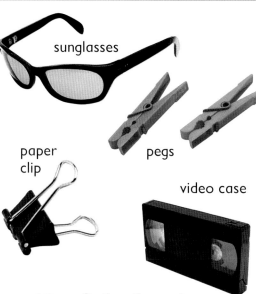

sunglasses

paper clip

pegs

video case

▲ Useful steel

Stainless steel is a very useful material because it does not rust easily. At a steelworks, the metal is heated to a high temperature and then welded into different shapes.

▼ Plants and animals

Many of the materials that we use every day come from plants or animals.

▲ Useful plastic

Look around and count how many plastic things you can see. The answer is probably 'lots'. Plastic is one of our most useful materials because we can make it into many different shapes. Plastic can be clear or coloured; it can bend and stretch and be hard or soft. Most plastic is made from petroleum.

wood, paper and rubber come from trees

the wool for a warm sweater comes from sheep or goats

the cotton to make a t-shirt comes from cotton plants

Wow!

A strong but lightweight metal called magnesium is found in seawater – we use it to make parts for cars and planes.

Word box

petroleum
a thick oil found under the ground or under the sea-bed

space shuttle
a spacecraft that can be used again and again

▶ Protective materials

The space shuttle becomes very, very hot when it returns to the Earth from space. The underneath part is covered with special tiles made from ceramic, a mixture of baked clay and other materials. The tiles protect the shuttle from the extreme heat.

▼

shuttle re-entering Earth's atmosphere

Measuring

Find out more:
Science ▶ Time ▶

Measuring helps you find the answer to questions such as 'How tall am I? How much do I weigh?' We use measurements all the time – in the kitchen, in shops, in the classroom, on a building site. We use many different tools to help us measure, such as scales and tape measures, clocks and thermometers, rulers and metre sticks.

▼ Hot and cold

A thermometer tells you how hot or cold something is – it measures temperature. A scale is marked along the side of the thermometer. Temperature is measured in degrees Celsius (°C) or Fahrenheit (°F).

▼ Telling the time

A clock tells you what time it is. We measure time in hours, minutes and seconds. The time of day is split into morning and afternoon – a.m. stands for morning and p.m. for afternoon.

▼ How long?

We use rulers or tape measures to find out how long something is. Every measurement consists of a number and a unit. If the side of a box measures 10 centimetres in length, then 10 is the number and centimetres (cm for short) is the unit of measurement.

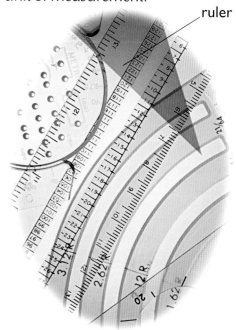

ruler

▼ How heavy?

Balances and scales help us to find out how heavy something is. The needle on the dial points to the correct weight.

Word box

scale
a row of steps or marks that are used for measuring something

Length and weight

This table explains units of length and weight. The units are sometimes shortened, or abbreviated, to save time and space. For example, mm is short for millimetre, and kg is short for kilogram.

Units of length
10 millimetres (mm) = 1 centimetre (cm)
100 cm = 1 metre (m)
1000 m = 1 kilometre (km)

Units of weight
1000 milligrams (mg) = 1 gram (g)
1000 g = 1 kilogram (kg)
1000 kg = 1 tonne (t)

Medicine

Find out more:
Jobs ◄ Science ► Scientists ► X-ray ►

Medicine is concerned with helping people who are ill or injured to get better. It is also involved with preventing the spread of serious infectious (spreading) illnesses such as measles, smallpox and malaria. Each year, new discoveries in medicine save more people's lives and find new ways to treat and cure illness.

▲ Hospitals

Sometimes you visit a hospital to receive treatment and then return home again. Some sick people stay in hospital to be looked after by the doctors and nurses who work there.

aloe vera

garlic

▲ Healing plants

Some plants are useful medicines too. Eating garlic is good for general health, and can help to keep your blood healthy. Aloe vera is used to treat skin conditions – it is a good treatment for sunburn too.

Wow!

In the Middle Ages many operations were carried out by barbers, not doctors – the barbers had plenty of sharp razors for cutting.

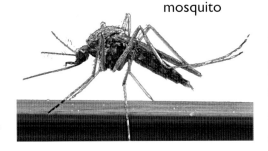

mosquito

▲ Stopping disease

Mosquitoes can spread a dangerous tropical disease called malaria, by biting human beings. Taking tablets can prevent the disease from developing. Other diseases can be prevented by giving special injections which are called vaccinations.

▼ Ancient medicine

Doctors have been treating sick people for thousands of years. In ancient Egypt, for example, doctors knew how to mend broken bones and treat stomach illnesses and eye infections. This doctor is treating a patient who is suffering with a skin complaint.

▼ Discovering medicine

In 1928, Alexander Fleming discovered a germ-killing medicine called penicillin. This discovery meant that many more infectious diseases could be treated and cured.

▼ Black Death

In the 1300s a terrible illness called the Black Death swept from one country to the next. It killed almost one-third of all the people in Europe. The disease was spread by black rats.

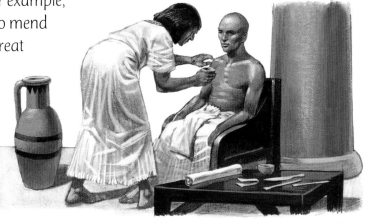

Money

We use money to buy things – from chocolate bars to computers, from toys to train tickets. Money can be in the form of paper notes or metal coins. We can also pay for something by writing a cheque or using a credit card.

▶ The first coins

The world's first coins were made about 2,500 years ago in a country called Lydia (part of modern Turkey). The coins, which were a mixture of gold and silver, had a design stamped on the front and back.

◀ Cash machines

You can collect money from a cashpoint machine. You insert a special card into the machine and key in your personal number. The machine, which is connected to your bank, gives you an amount of cash. The same amount is then taken out of your bank account.

▼ Making money

Money is made in a special factory called a mint. In the past, coins were made from gold, silver and other expensive metals. Modern coins are made from a mixture of metals such as zinc, nickel and copper.

Word scramble

Can you match each of these currencies with the correct country they are used in?

1. LIRA   a. GREAT BRITAIN
2. YEN   b. SPAIN
3. PESETA   c. JAPAN
4. DOLLAR   d. ITALY
5. POUND   e. UNITED STATES

answers
1d 2c 3b 4e 5a

▲ Money names

Each country has its own money, called a currency. The currency of the United States is the US dollar. The currency of France is the French franc. What is the currency of your country?

Moon

The Moon is our closest neighbour – it is nearer to the Earth than any other object in space. The Moon travels around the Earth and takes about one month to make a complete journey. The Moon seems to be shining because it reflects light from the Sun.

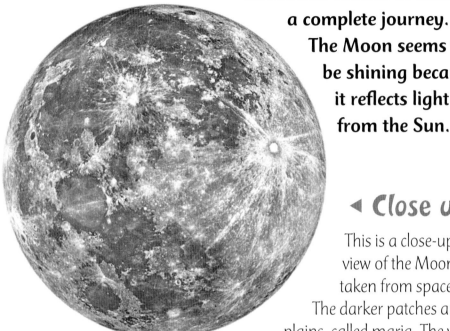

◀ Close up

This is a close-up view of the Moon taken from space. The darker patches are plains, called maria. The word 'maria' means seas, but there is no water on the Moon. The lighter areas are highlands. There are also lots of craters on the surface of the Moon.

▲ In the shadows

When the Moon passes into the Earth's shadow, it is called a lunar (Moon) eclipse. The Moon grows darker and redder. A solar (Sun) eclipse is when the Moon passes between the Earth and the Sun, blocking the Sun's light (above).

▼ Changing shape

The Moon seems to change shape from day to day. It takes 28.73 days to pass through all these changes, which we call phases. Sometimes we see just a tiny slice of the Moon – this is because the rest of the Moon is in darkness.

new Moon

crescent Moon

first quarter

gibbous Moon

full Moon

Word box

crater
a dent in the ground

plain
a wide, flat area

▶ Moon walk

The *Apollo 11* spacecraft landed on the Moon on July 20, 1969. Two astronauts stepped onto the Moon's surface – the first humans to walk on the Moon.

Mountains

Find out more:
North America ▶ Rivers and lakes ▶
Rocks and minerals ▶

Sharp peaks covered with ice and snow, long steep slopes, rivers that flow quickly, rocky valleys – these are just some of the sights you might see in the mountains. A mountain is usually much higher than the land around it. When several mountains are grouped together they form a mountain range. The Alps in Europe are an example of this.

▼ Mountain forms

There are three main ways in which mountains are formed.

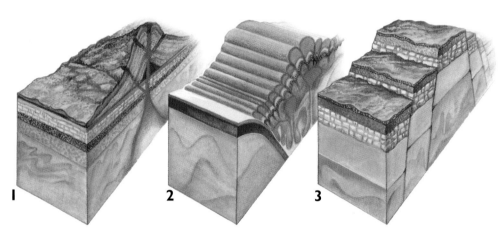

1. volcanoes form mountains when lava inside the Earth cools and hardens

2. layers of rocks are forced up into 'folds'

3. rocks may crack, causing faults, allowing large areas of rock to be pushed up

Word scramble

Unscramble these words to find the names of five large mountain ranges:

a. SPAL
b. SKICORE
c. NASED
d. ASLAMYAIH
e. SALTA

answers
a. ALPS b. ROCKIES c. ANDES
d. HIMALAYAS e. ATLAS

▲ Mountain range

A group of mountain ranges called the Alps stretches across parts of France, Italy, Switzerland and Austria. The Alps are very popular for winter sports, such as skiing.

▼ Mountain life

This mountain goat has a thick coat to keep it warm, and feet that are good for climbing in rocky places.

▼ The Rockies

The Rocky Mountains run for about 3,000 kilometres down the west coast of North America. There are several national parks and ski resorts in the spectacular scenery.

▼ Top of the world

For hundreds of years people have enjoyed climbing mountains. In 1953 two climbers reached the top of the world's highest mountain, Mount Everest, in Asia. They were Edmund Hillary from New Zealand, and Tenzing Norgay, his guide.

Music

You can hear the sounds of music almost everywhere you go. Music can be a pop song on the radio, a choir singing in church, an orchestra performing, someone playing the piano in a café or restaurant, a band marching through the street. We listen to music to enjoy ourselves and to relax. It also plays an important part in many festivals and religious ceremonies.

Wow!

The Austrian composer Wolfgang Amadeus Mozart composed his first piece of music at the age of five.

◄ Playing music

Music is played on instruments such as the piano, recorder or clarinet. Many children learn to play a musical instrument at school. Can you play any of these instruments?

▲ Different sounds

There are many different sounds and styles of music throughout the world. This is a gamelan orchestra from Indonesia, in southeast Asia. Gamelan orchestras often play their music for shadow puppet plays in puppet theatres.

trumpet

flute

violin

Beethoven

◄ Composing music

A composer is someone who writes music. Beethoven (1770–1827) was a famous German composer. He wrote and played music even though he began to go deaf.

▲ Electronic sounds

Many modern musicians use electronic instruments to create sounds in recording studios. These instruments, called synthesizers, can copy perfectly the sound of, say, a drum or a guitar.

Word box

orchestra
large group of musicians playing different instruments

shadow puppet
a puppet held behind a screen that is lit up

► Drum music

Steel drums are popular in the West Indies. The drums are made from empty oil drums and make a lively ringing sound. Drummers play them with bare hands or with padded sticks.

▼

North America

North America is made up of the three large countries of Canada, the United States of America and Mexico, as well as a number of smaller countries. These smaller nations include the island of Greenland, the small countries of Central America and the islands dotted around the Caribbean Sea.

▼ Tallest trees

Thick forests of huge redwoods, cedars, firs and spruces can be found in California and Oregon.

These huge trees thrive on mountain side slopes which face the Pacific Ocean. Redwoods are the tallest living things and can grow to heights of 80 metres.

▶ From north to south

In the far north of the continent of North America are the frozen lands of Alaska, which border the Arctic Ocean. Mountains run down both the east and west sides of the continent, with wide plains, long rivers and large lakes in the centre. In the far south are the sandy beaches of the Caribbean islands and the hot, wet jungles of Central America.

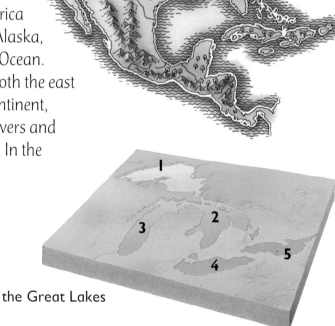

the Great Lakes

◀ Very deep

In the southwest of the continent is the amazing Grand Canyon, the deepest canyon in the world. This steep-sided valley was carved out by the Colorado River over millions of years.

▲ Great Lakes

On the border between Canada and the United States are the five Great Lakes: **1** Superior, **2** Huron, **3** Erie, **4** Ontario, **5** Michigan. Together these lakes make up the largest body of fresh water to be found anywhere in the world. Lake Superior is the biggest of all fresh water lakes.

North American life

North America is a land of different peoples. It includes some of the world's biggest and most famous cities, such as New York, Los Angeles and Mexico City.

Many North Americans are descended from Europeans, who began settling here in the 1500s. The people who were already living here are called Native Americans.

Wow!

New York's Statue of Liberty was built in France and then transported to the United States in 214 separate wooden crates.

▲ Skyscraper city

The skyscrapers of Los Angeles crowd against the city's night skyline. Los Angeles is the second largest city in the United States, after New York City. The city's tallest building, The Library Tower, is 310 meters high.

▼ Playing baseball

Baseball is one of the most popular sports in the United States. Millions of people watch games each week, either live at their local ballpark or on television.

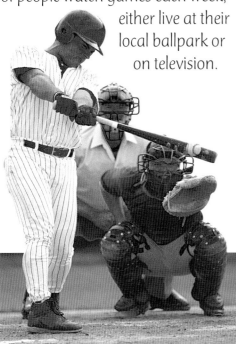

▲ Space centre

American spacecraft are launched into space from Cape Canaveral, on the coast of Florida, in the southeast of the United States. The first spacecraft to land on the Moon lifted off from here in 1969.

▼ Fast sport

Ice hockey is the national game of Canada, and every week thousands of people turn out to watch their favourite teams. Ice hockey is a very fast sport and the players wear protective clothing.

▼ Cities and temples

The ruins of ancient Aztec cities are scattered across Mexico. The Aztec people built cities filled with beautiful temples and buildings. In the 1500s, Spanish invaders conquered the Aztecs and destroyed their empire.

Oceania

Australia is by far the largest country in the continent of Oceania. The two other sizeable countries are New Zealand and Papua New Guinea. The rest of Oceania is made up of hundreds of islands in the Pacific Ocean.

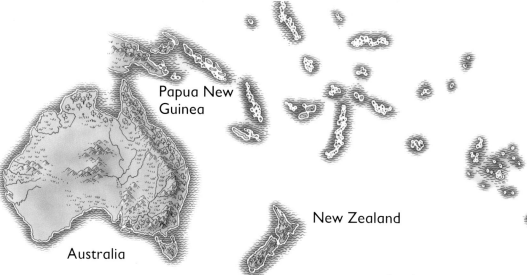

Papua New Guinea

Australia

New Zealand

▲ Hot and dry

Away from its coasts, much of Australia is covered by huge areas of open land. These are called the Outback. They are mostly hot desert areas and dry grasslands.

▲ Island continent

The land of Australia is mostly flat. In the east, mountains separate the dry inland areas from a narrow strip of fertile land along the coast. New Zealand is made up of two islands: North Island and South Island. High mountain peaks, active volcanoes, hot, bubbling springs and green lowlands are to be found on the islands. Mountains and thick forests cover much of Papua New Guinea, Oceania's third largest country.

coral polyps

▲ The largest reef

The Great Barrier Reef lies off the northeastern coast of Australia. It is the world's largest coral reef and stretches for 2,000 kilometres. Coral is made up of the skeletons of tiny sea animals called polyps.

▶ Koalas

The koala is one of Australia's most famous animals. It eats only one kind of food – the young leaves and shoots of eucalyptus trees. Like a kangaroo, a koala mother keeps her baby in a pouch on her stomach.

▶ Active volcanoes

On the small islands around New Zealand can be found active volcanoes. This means there is a chance they could erupt. This volcano is on White Island, and it often gives off smoke.

Oceania and its people

Oceania covers a large area of the world but only about 30 million people live there. Around 19 million people live in Australia – that's roughly the same as live in the tiny country of Nepal in Asia. Most Australians live along the coast, where there is plenty of rain. The two largest cities – Sydney and Melbourne – are in this coastal strip. There are few towns in the huge inland part of Australia.

▲ Sacred rock

Uluru is a sacred place for the Aborigines, the native people of Australia. Called Ayers Rock in English, it is the largest rock in the world. Inside the rock are many caves. Their walls are covered with paintings made by Aboriginal artists thousands of years ago.

Word box

Aboriginal
original inhabitant

landmark
a famous sight

sacred
holy, very special

▲ First to arrive

The Maoris were the first inhabitants (settlers) of New Zealand. They came by canoe around AD800 from islands far to the northeast. Europeans arrived in the late 1700s. Maoris are skilled woodcarvers and stone sculptors.

▼ Sydney harbour

The Opera House (completed in 1973) in Sydney's great harbour is Australia's most famous landmark. Sydney is Australia's biggest city – one-fifth of all Australians live here.

Wow!

The first people from Europe to settle in Australia were prisoners and their guards from England – they sailed there in 11 ships in 1787.

▼ Rugby fans

Australians and New Zealanders are very keen on sport and other outdoor activities. The game of rugby is very popular in both countries. The New Zealand team is known as the 'All-Blacks' because of the colour they wear.

Oceans and life

Find out more:
Animal kingdom ◄ Fish ◄ Oceans and seas ►
Water ►

The oceans are filled with living things. These range from the tiny shrimp-like creatures that float on the surface to strange-looking fish that crawl across the sea-bed. Most ocean creatures live in the warmer, sunlit waters near the surface, where most of their food supply is found.

▼ Floating life

Tiny plants and animals called plankton drift across the surface of the water in huge numbers. They become food for larger ocean creatures.

▼ Ocean creatures

Sharks, dolphins and turtles live near the water's surface. Large mammals such as the sei whale dive to lower levels. The waters at the bottom of the ocean receive almost no sunlight. Only a few kinds of sea creatures can survive in this cold, dark world.

1 dusky dolphin	8 sunfish	14 banded sea snake
2 kittiwake	9 turtle	15 tuna
3 right whale	10 cuttlefish	16 squid
4 jellyfish	11 tiger shark	17 mako shark
5 great skuas	12 yellow-bellied	18 nautilus
6 common dolphin	sea snake	19 white-sided dolphin
7 broad-billed prion	13 tarpon	20 sei whale

Oceans and seas

Find out more:
Earth features ◄ Oceans and life ◄
Water ►

Oceans and seas cover more than two-thirds of the Earth's surface. Amazingly, they contain 97 percent of all the water in the world. The oceans are about four kilometres deep on average, but in some places the ocean floor plunges down even deeper. The deepest place in the world is at the bottom of the Pacific Ocean – the Marianas Trench is more than 11 kilometres below the water's surface.

Wow!

In May 1985, a tsunami struck the shores of Bangladesh, killing more than 10,000 people.

► Ocean waters

There are five great oceans, which are joined together by smaller seas and other stretches of water. From largest to smallest, the oceans are: the Pacific, the Atlantic, the Indian, the Arctic and the Southern.

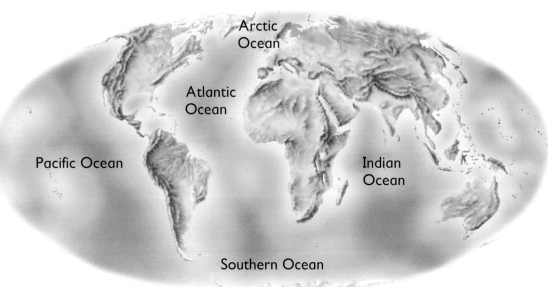

Arctic Ocean

Atlantic Ocean

Pacific Ocean

Indian Ocean

Southern Ocean

► Moving water

The water in our oceans and seas is always moving. As wind blows across the water's surface, it creates waves. Waves move around the world in swirling, circular patterns called currents.

surface currents

underwater currents

wave movement

▼ Giant waves

Earthquakes under the sea-bed can produce giant waves that race towards land at speeds as fast as 970 kilometres per hour. They are called *tsunamis*.

◄ Fish to eat

Each year, humans take millions of tonnes of fish and shellfish from the world's oceans and seas. In some places people have caught too many fish, and supplies of some kinds are now running out.

Oil and gas

Find out more:
Electricity ◄ Energy ◄ Pollution ►

We use oil and gas to power our cars, planes and trains, to heat our homes, and to make electricity. Oil supplies about half of all the energy we use in the world. We find oil and gas in rocks deep under the ground or below the sea-bed.

▲ Out at sea

This oil rig is floating in the middle of the sea off the coast of Scotland. Special anchor ropes hold the rig in place. Oil workers sleep, eat and work on the rig or on a separate rig nearby. They travel to and from the rig by helicopter.

► Transporting oil

The oil taken from under the ground or under the sea is called crude oil. It is transported along a pipeline or by a tanker. The tanker may be a ship, lorry or part of a train. The oil is taken to a refinery where it is turned into petrol for cars, diesel fuel for lorries and buses, and lots of other useful substances.

▼ Burning gas

We burn gas to heat our homes and for cooking. Gas comes into our homes through pipes under the ground. Many factories use gas to heat and cut metals.

► Useful products

Plastic items, lipstick, soap powder, fertilizer, nylon and paint – these are just some of the many things we make from oil.

soap powder

paint

plastic cutlery set

lipstick

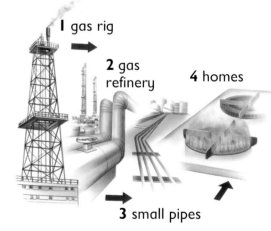

1 gas rig

2 gas refinery

4 homes

3 small pipes

◄ Running out

Almost half of the world's crude oil is used to make fuel for cars and small planes. But one day this oil will run out. Scientists think that there is possibly only enough oil to last for another 50 or 60 years.

Wow!
The Trans Alaska Pipeline in North America crosses three mountain ranges, hundreds of kilometres of frozen ground and 300 rivers and streams.

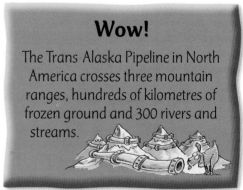

Planets

Mercury

Venus

Earth

Mars

Our Earth is one of a family of nine planets that travel around the Sun. Each planet moves along its own oval-shaped path, called an orbit. Spacecraft from the Earth have visited every planet except Pluto, the farthest planet from the Sun. No humans have ever landed on another planet – yet!

▲ Rings of colour

Saturn is surrounded by thousands of beautiful coloured rings. The rings are really tiny pieces of ice, rock and dust. There are more moons travelling around Saturn than any other planet – 23 that we know about, and perhaps even more.

► Planet-spotting

You can see five of the planets from the Earth without a telescope: Mercury, Venus, Mars, Jupiter and Saturn. Venus is the brightest of these, and you can see it shining low down in the morning sky just before the Sun rises. We often call Venus the 'morning star'.

Jupiter

Saturn

Uranus

Neptune

Pluto

▼ Landing on Mars

A spacecraft called *Pathfinder* landed on Mars in 1997. Inside it was a robot vehicle, which travelled across the planet's surface. The robot collected rock samples and took photographs.

Pathfinder

► Ball of rock

The surface of Mars is covered with red dust and rocks. Mars is one of the rocky planets, like the Earth. Venus, Mercury and Pluto are also rocky planets.

▼

Planet search

The names of five planets are hidden in this grid. Can you find them?

V	E	L	S	J	U	T	K
I	S	P	A	B	N	R	U
P	L	U	T	O	L	E	M
A	Y	R	U	D	Q	A	B
L	M	E	R	C	U	R	Y
J	A	K	N	O	F	T	E
P	R	I	N	L	A	H	T
O	S	M	E	F	S	E	R

answers: PLUTO, MERCURY, MARS, SATURN, EARTH

Plants

Find out more:
Flowers ◄ Trees ► Plants around the world ►

Plants grow all around you – in the garden and in the park, on the window-sill, in the farmer's fields, in woods and forests, on rocks and cliffs – even on the beach. The biggest plants are giant sequoia trees that tower more than 80 metres above the ground. The smallest ones are hairy mosses that spread like a carpet over rocks and stones.

Word box

germination
the stages of seed growth

photosynthesis
the way in which plants make food

▲ Mossy rocks

These rocks have turned green with moss, a tiny plant that grows in large numbers. Most mosses live in moist, shady places, and form soft 'mats' over rocks and around the bases of trees.

▼ Life underground

Once a seed has found a suitable place, it begins to grow. This process is called germination.

1. the seed lies in the ground until conditions are right

2. the seed sends a shoot up and a root down

3. the shoot pushes its way above ground

▶ Making food

Green plants make their own food by using light from the Sun. This process is called photosynthesis. It happens inside the plant's leaves. A special substance in the leaves uses water from the soil, carbon dioxide gas from the air and sunlight to make food. The food travels through the stems to reach all parts of the plant.

carbon dioxide is taken in

sunlight

oxygen is given out

water taken up by the roots

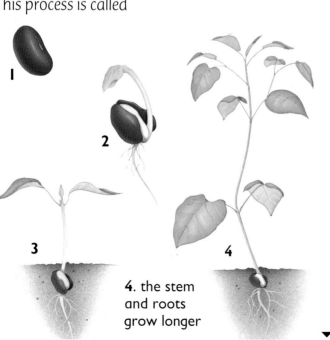

1

2

3

4. the stem and roots grow longer

Grow your own bean sprouts

Crunchy bean sprouts are delicious to eat – and you can grow them yourself. Put a handful of beans, such as aduki beans, into a clean jam jar and cover the jar entrance with a sheet of thick paper towel. Hold in place with a rubber band. Carefully pour enough warm water through the paper towel to cover the beans. Leave for 12 hours, then empty the water without taking out the paper towel. Repeat every day for 4 to 5 days until you have enough bean sprouts to eat. They taste delicious!

Plants around the world

Find out more:
Antarctica ◄ Deserts ◄
Plants ◄

Plants include trees with cones, plants with showy, colourful flowers, grasses, ferns and small plants such as mosses and liverworts. Plants grow in almost every corner of the world – mosses grow in the freezing cold Antarctic and cacti grow in hot, dry deserts. Other plants prefer swampy marshland or hot, wet rainforests.

► Hot and dry

Desert plants have to survive in extreme heat with very little or no water. Cacti are well suited to life in the desert. They store water in their thick, fleshy stems. Some cactuses have roots that spread a long way just below the surface so they can quickly take in water after a shower of rain.

bristlecone pine

► In the cold

Most plants which live in very cold places have hairy leaves or hard shiny ones. These help the plant to keep in as much water as possible. Arctic cotton grass can be found in icy Arctic conditions. It covers the ground in spring.

◄ Ancient trees

Scientists have already found at least 350,000 different kinds of plant. The oldest living things in the world are plants. A bristlecone pine tree in California, USA is at least 4,000 years old already.

▲ Big flowers

The sunflower is a very tall plant and can measure between one and three metres in height. Its brightly coloured head (flower) is recognised and grown all over the world. A single flower can be up to 30 centimetres in width. Sunflower heads are a rich source of seeds, and these are used in the production of vegetable oil, for cooking and margarine.

Wow!

The seeds of the coco-de-mer tree, which grows on islands in the Indian Ocean, weigh up to 20 kilograms each – that's about the same as a medium-sized dog.

Pollution

Litter in the street, dirty smoke and gases in the air, dangerous chemicals in rivers and streams – all these are examples of pollution. Pollution is the waste products that damage the air, the land and the water around us. It can kill plants and animals, make humans beings ill and even damage old buildings.

Word box

soot
the black powder found in smoke from a chimney

transport
to move from one place to another

▲ Oil disaster

Oil is transported across the sea by tankers. Sometimes a tanker is involved in an accident, leading to an oil spillage. This can have a devastating effect, killing marine life for miles around. Oil is also washed up on beaches, and cleaning up can take months, even years.

Wow!

If we recycled three-quarters of all the paper in the world, we would save more than 35 million trees every year.

► Into the water

All over the world, people pour harmful waste into streams, lakes and rivers. This water pollution kills fish and the water plants they feed on, and makes the water unsafe for people to drink.

▲ Dirty air

The gases from car exhausts fill our cities with soot, smoke and other dirt. This dirty air can harm people's eyes and make it difficult for them to breathe. By using cleaner fuel, people can help to reduce the level of polluted air.

▼ Using again

We can reduce the amount of waste from our homes by recycling it. Recycling means turning an old product into another material and using it again. You can recycle glass bottles and jars, newspapers and cardboard, drinks and food cans, plastic bottles and old clothing.

Prehistoric life

Find out more:
Art and painting ◀ Dinosaurs ◀

**The first human beings lived on Earth
a long time ago – around 2 million years ago.**
At this time most of the world was cold and icy, but Africa,
South America and parts of Asia were warmer. These early
people learned how to make fire, hunted animals and
made simple tools from wood, stone
and animal bones.

Word box

bison
huge prehistoric cattle

prehistoric
the time before history
was written down

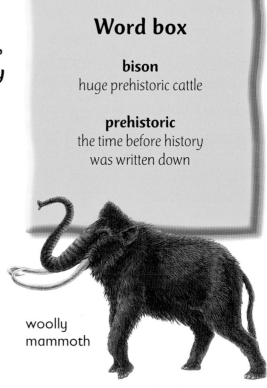
woolly
mammoth

▲ Making fire

The earliest use of fire-making was
for warmth. But people eventually
discovered the uses of fire – for
cooking, to shape weapons and
tools, and to give light.

▼ A long time ago

The word 'prehistoric' means the
time before people could write.
It is the time before about
5,000 years ago. This period of
prehistory is called the Stone Age.
People made their own tools and
weapons out
of stone.

this stone tool
was used for scraping
flesh from the skin of
wild animals

▲ Mammoth hunts

Early people hunted birds, small
reptiles and larger animals such as
deer, bison, bears and huge
elephant-like animals called woolly
mammoths.

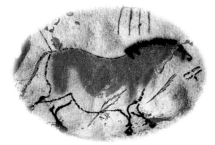

▲ Cave art

Prehistoric people painted pictures
of animals and everyday life on
cave walls. The first person to
find any of these pictures was a
12-year-old Spanish girl, more
than 100 years ago.

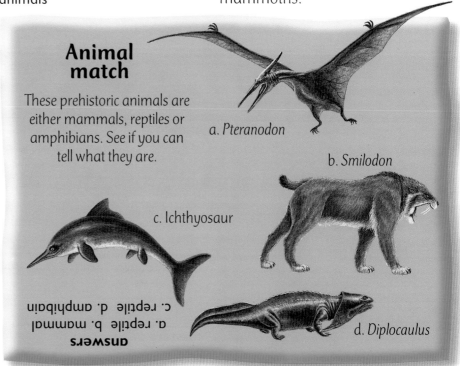

Animal match

These prehistoric animals are
either mammals, reptiles or
amphibians. See if you can
tell what they are.

a. *Pteranodon*

b. *Smilodon*

c. Ichthyosaur

d. *Diplocaulus*

answers
a. reptile b. mammal
c. reptile d. amphibian

Queens

Find out more:
Egyptians ◀ Kings ◀

A queen is either the ruler of a country or she is the wife of a king. In history, several powerful queens have reigned for many years. Elizabeth I ruled England for 45 years. She beat off an invasion by a fleet of ships from Spain, and kept tight control over her country.

Elizabeth I

Wow!

People tried to kill Queen Victoria on six different occasions.

◀ Poisoned queen

Cleopatra was queen of ancient Egypt when the country was under the control of the Romans. She was a very ambitious and determined queen. According to legend, Cleopatra killed herself by letting a poisonous snake bite her arm.

▼ Queen Victoria

Queen Victoria was such an important queen that her name is used to describe a whole period in Britain's history – the Victorian Age. She reigned for 63 years, from 1837 to 1901, and had nine children. While she was queen, Britain became one of the world's richest and most powerful countries.

▶ Warrior queen

About 950 years ago a queen called Boudicca ruled the Iceni tribe in Britain. She led her army against the Romans. Boudicca and her soldiers destroyed Roman towns and killed many soldiers. She poisoned herself to avoid capture.

◀ In Europe

Several European countries are ruled by queens, but none of them has any real power to make decisions. A queen has ruled the Netherlands since 1890. The present one, Queen Beatrix, became queen in 1980.

Rainforests

Find out more:
Conservation ◀ Forests ◀ South America ▶ Trees ▶

Rainforests are thick forests of tall trees that grow in hot, rainy parts of the world. These forests stay green all year round. The largest rainforest of all, the Amazon, takes up one-third of the continent of South America. Many thousands of different kinds of animals and plants live in rainforests.

▼ Top to bottom

A rainforest is packed with life. The treetops form a covering, called the canopy. Eagles(1), monkeys (2), butterflies (3) and macaws (4) live in the canopy. Sloths (5) hang from the middle branches, and jaguars (6) climb into lower branches. On the forest floor, millipedes (7) and beetles (8) move through the leaves.

▶ Bright colours

Many rainforest animals are very colourful, like this orange bird wing butterfly. Its colours warn other animals that it is not good to eat.

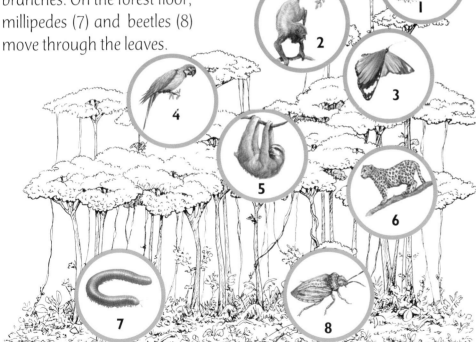

Wow!
Every second, humans cut down an area of tropical rainforest that measures the same size as a football pitch.

▼ Destruction

Farmers clear land in rainforests by cutting down trees and burning them. The soil in many rainforests is poor, and after a few years the farmers' crops no longer grow well. This means they have to clear another patch of rainforest. In this way people are destroying large areas of the world's rainforests.

◀ Forest life

A small number of people still follow a traditional way of life in some of the world's rainforests. These South American Indians speak their own language and hunt for food.

Religion

A religion is a set of ideas and beliefs, which usually centre around one god or several gods. There are more than 1,000 different religions in the world. They have their own ceremonies and festivals, where

followers often come together to worship the god of their religion. In most religions, people come to a special place, such as a church, a temple or a synagogue, to pray and worship.

Wow!

At their spring festival of Holi, Hindu people spray each other with coloured powder or water.

▼ Jerusalem

The city of Jerusalem is a holy place for three different religious groups: Christians, Muslims and Jews. These Jewish people are praying at the Western Wall in Jerusalem. This is the only part left of the temple where Jesus prayed.

▲ In nature

Shinto is a religion of Japan. Its followers believe that good spirits live in the natural world – in rocks and mountains, in forests and rivers, in animals and trees.

the Pope is based at the Vatican, the smallest state in the world, in the city of Rome, Italy

▲ Religious leaders

Religious leaders can have many different names, according to the religion they represent – monk, priest, imam and rabbi are some of the most common ones. The Pope is the head of the Roman Catholic Church, which is a branch of the Christian religion.

▼ Holy place

In India, Sikhs are a group of people who believe in one God. They follow special teachings and are taught to lead simple lives. The Golden Temple at Amritsar is their most important holy place.

▲ Finding peace

This Buddhist temple is in Bangkok, Thailand. Buddhists follow the ideas of Buddha, an Indian prince who lived about 2,500 years ago. He believed that people could find peace and happiness if they followed a certain way of life.

Word box

holy
very religious

synagogue
a building where Jews worship

Religion and people

Find out more:
Asian people ◄ Religion ◄

**Each religion has its own group of followers –
Christians, Hindus, Buddhists, Muslims and
Jews are some of the best-known ones.** Many
believers follow the rules of their religion very strictly.
For example Muslims, who follow the religion of Islam,
must pray five times each day: at sunrise, at midday,
in the afternoon, in the evening and at sunset.

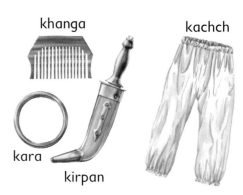

khanga

kachch

kara

kirpan

▶ Holy waters

The ancient religion of Hinduism is
at least 4,000 years old. More than
three-quarters of the people in India
are Hindus. The river Ganges in
India is a very holy place for them.
Pilgrims come from all over India to
bathe in its waters. By doing this
they wash away their sins, and
become pure.

▲ Religious symbols

The Sikh religion was founded in
the Punjab area of India in the
1500s. Spiritual teachers set guide
lines on how people should lead
their lives. Male followers of the
religion wear the five 'Ks'– kesh
(uncut hair), khanga (comb),
kirpan (sword), kara (steel bangle)
and kachch (shorts).

▼ All together

People do not always have to go to a special place or building to pray.
This American religious leader is holding a service in front of a huge
crowd of people gathered in the open. Millions of others also watch the
service on their televisions.

▲ Muslims at Mecca

The holiest place for Muslims is the
city of Mecca in Saudi Arabia.
Inside the Great Mosque is a black
stone, which Muslims believe came
from their God, whom they call
Allah. All Muslims try to visit
Mecca at least once in their life.
Around one million people crowd
into the city each year during the
six days set aside for this visit.

Reptiles

Find out more:
Animal kingdom ◀ Dinosaurs ◀
Reptiles of the world ▶

Alligators and crocodiles, lizards and snakes, tortoises and turtles are different kinds of reptile. Most reptiles have a dry skin covered with tough scales. Reptiles are cold-blooded, which means they lie in the sun to warm up before they can move around. There are about 6,000 different kinds of reptile.

Word box

flesh
the soft part of a body under the skin

snout
the nose and mouth parts of an animal

▲ Slow movers

Tortoises are very slow-moving reptiles. They live on land, whereas turtles live in water. Some live for over 150 years. The world's largest tortoise comes from the island of Aldabra off the coast of East Africa. It can reach 1.8 metres in length.

agama lizard

▲ Warming up

This lizard is warming its body in the sunshine. Unlike mammals, including humans, reptiles are cold-blooded. This means they have to bask in the sun to warm up and make themselves active. If they get too hot, they have to scuttle into some shade.

grass snake

▼ Fierce hunters

Alligators and crocodiles are fierce hunters with huge, sharp teeth. They use these teeth to hold onto prey in the water and to tear flesh. Their tails are long and powerful, helping them to swim swiftly. An alligator has a shorter, squarer snout than a crocodile.

◀ Egg layers

Most reptiles lay their eggs in a warm, dry place. The heat of the sunshine makes the eggs hatch. A mother grass snake may lay her eggs in compost or manure heaps. The heat given off by these heaps helps to speed up the development of the eggs.

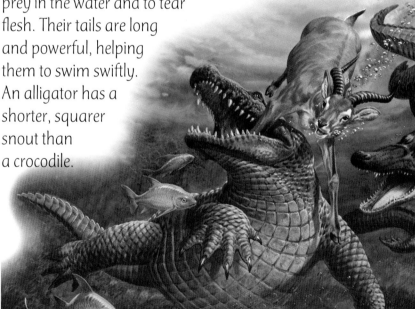

Reptiles of the world

Find out more:
Animal kingdom ◄
Dinosaurs ◄ Reptiles ◄

Reptiles live in most places, except in the very cold areas in the far north and far south of the world. Many snakes and lizards live in hot deserts. Some kinds of reptile, such as sea turtles, spend most of their life in the water.

tree gecko

► On the beach

Mother sea turtles come onto land to lay their eggs. They bury the eggs in a hole in a sandy beach and then go back to the sea. When the baby turtles hatch, they make their own way to the water. They have to avoid the hungry birds and crabs waiting to catch them.

▲ Sticky feet

The gecko is a lizard found in most warm countries. The biggest gecko lives in Southeast Asia and can be 30 centimetres in length. The tree gecko has hairs on its feet, which have a sticking effect. This enables it to walk on any surface, and even hang on by just one toe!

▼ Like a dinosaur

The tuatara lives on the islands of New Zealand. It belongs to a group of reptiles called 'beak heads', and first lived around the time of the dinosaurs, reptiles that roamed the Earth millions of years ago.

◄ Skin change

Many snakes, such as this grass snake, get rid of the skin on their body several times each year. The new skin grows under the old one and makes it loose. When the new skin is ready, the snake wriggles out of the old one.

► Dragon lizards

The Komodo dragon is the largest lizard and can grow up to three metres in length. It lives on small islands in Indonesia. These lizards are very fierce, and will eat almost anything. Perhaps that's how they got their dragon name!

Wow!

A lizard that lives in the forests of Asia can glide from tree to tree through the air — it is known as a 'flying dragon'.

Rivers and lakes

Find out more:
Egyptians ◄ Energy sources ◄
Oceans and seas ◄ Water ►

source

delta

river mouth

A river makes a long journey from its beginning, to the place where it empties into the sea, a lake or another river. Rivers provide us with water for drinking and washing and to water our crops. They also supply us with fish to eat. Rivers are important travel routes, and many towns and cities have grown up beside a river.

▲ Start to finish

The place where a river starts is called its source. It is often high up in the mountains, where melting snows begin to trickle downhill. Near the source, the land is often steep and the river is quite narrow, so its waters flow quickly. Lower down, the river becomes wider and flows more slowly and smoothly.

► Masses of water

The huge Amazon river in South America carries more water than any other river in the world. It is so wide in places that if you stand on one bank you cannot see the river bank on the opposite side.

▼ Water sport

Fast-flowing rivers are exciting places for canoeists. Paddling through fast water is often called 'shooting the rapids'.

◄ Making a lake

A lake is an area of water with land all around it. Some very large lakes are actually called seas, for example the Dead Sea and the Caspian Sea. This is Lake Kariba in southern Africa. It is an artificial lake, which was made by blocking the waters of the Zambezi river.

Word box

artificial
made by people

rapids
part of a river where water moves quickly and dangerously

◄ Shopping by boat

In parts of Asia, people use waterways to buy and sell food. These Chinese people have come by boat to shop at a floating market.

Word scramble

Can you unscramble these words to find the names of five large rivers?

**a. SMATHE
b. NIHER
c. ZANAMO
d. ISPISIMISPS
e. SGEGNA**

answers
a. Thames b. Rhine
c. Amazon d. Mississippi
e. Ganges

Roads

Millions of motor cars, buses and lorries travel along roads each day. Fast, straight roads called motorways link cities and large towns together. In the countryside, small narrow roads run between villages. About 2,000 years ago, the Romans built paved roads across parts of Europe and North Africa.

▼ Building a road

To make a new road, huge earth-moving machines are used to cut away earth, flatten surfaces and smooth concrete.

▲ Roman roads

The Romans built long, straight roads covered with flat stones, such as this one in Algeria, North Africa. They used these roads to move soldiers quickly from place to place.

1. a bulldozer pushes away earth

2. a scraper levels the ground and smooths a path

3. a dumptruck brings crushed rock

4. a grader smooths rocks to make a flat base

5. a paving machine spreads on a mixture of sand, stones and tar (asphalt), which is then rolled by a rolling machine

◄ So many roads

We are building more roads to cope with the increasing amounts of traffic. Motorways can help to take the strain of all this traffic away from smaller roads, where traffic jams may begin.

▼ Heavy loads

You see many huge lorries like this one on motorways and other fast roads. They transport large loads, often from one country to another. These very large lorries are called 'juggernauts'.

Wow!
The world's longest truck, the Arctic Snow Train, is over 170 metres long, has 54 wheels and needs a team of six drivers.

Rocks and minerals

Rocks are the hard, solid parts of the Earth's surface. You can see them on hillsides and in mountains and river valleys. The tall cliffs at the seaside are made of rock. In other places you cannot see rocks because they are covered by soil and trees, grass and other plants. Every kind of rock is made up of smaller pieces called minerals.

► Buried treasure

Gold is a precious mineral that is found inside rocks, deep under the ground. Silver and quartz are other common minerals.

Word box

mineral
very small pieces of rock

monument
something built in memory of a special person or event

▼ Beautiful marble

A rock called marble comes in different colours and patterns. The ancient Greeks carved statues out of marble. Today, we use it for buildings, floor and wall tiles, as well as for monuments. The Taj Mahal in India (right) has beautiful marble detail.

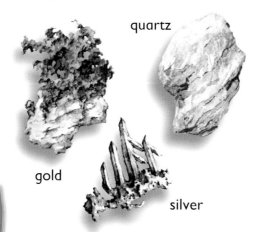

quartz

gold

silver

▼ Diamonds

Diamond is the hardest substance in nature. This mineral is used in industry for cutting. Cut diamonds sparkle so brightly that they make valuable gemstones.

▼ Rare minerals

Some minerals are very rare and beautiful — and expensive too! We call them gemstones, or gems for short. Rubies, emeralds and sapphires are well-known gems that we make into jewellery and ornaments.

rubies

Wow!

About three-quarters of all the gold produced in the world each year comes from South Africa.

▼ Giant's rocks

The Giant's Causeway in Northern Ireland is made up of thousands of pillars of a black rock called basalt. It formed when hot, liquid rocks from deep inside the Earth gushed out onto the surface and then cooled and gradually hardened.

Match the names

Do you know the most common colour of these gemstones? Match the name of each gem with the correct colour.

1. emerald
2. sapphire
3. ruby
4. pearl
5. topaz

a. blue
b. yellow
c. white
d. green
e. red

answers
1d 2a 3e 4c 5b

Romans

Find out more:
Roads ◄ Volcanoes ►

The ancient Romans came from Italy. From about 250 BC to 300 AD, they spread their way of life across Europe, the Middle East and parts of North Africa. The soldiers of the vast Roman army conquered many lands and peoples. The Romans were great engineers and builders, and they made laws that many European countries still follow today.

► At the baths

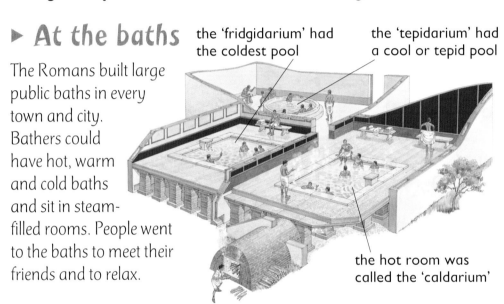

the 'fridgidarium' had the coldest pool

the 'tepidarium' had a cool or tepid pool

the hot room was called the 'caldarium'

The Romans built large public baths in every town and city. Bathers could have hot, warm and cold baths and sit in steam-filled rooms. People went to the baths to meet their friends and to relax.

▲ Eruption!

Almost 2,000 years ago, the entire Roman town of Pompeii was buried under hot ashes when the volcano of Vesuvius erupted in AD79. Since the 1700s, many bodies and buildings have been uncovered. These have told historians a great deal about how people lived in the Roman empire.

▼ Using numbers

The Romans wrote numbers by using symbols. Each Roman numeral was made up of different combinations of these seven symbols: I (1), V (5), X (10), L (50), C (100), D (500) and M (1,000). The Roman numeral for 1, 556 is: MDLVI (1,000 + 500 + 50 + 5 + 1).

▼ Skilled fighters

Roman soldiers were skilled and well-trained fighters. When they were not fighting wars, soldiers helped to build roads, bridges and forts.

Word box

conquer
to overcome or defeat

erupt
to shoot out hot rocks and gases

Wow!

The Romans set aside 135 days of each year for holidays and festivals – that's more than one-third of a year!

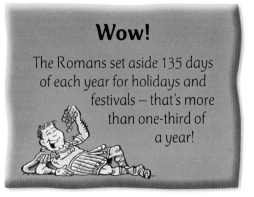

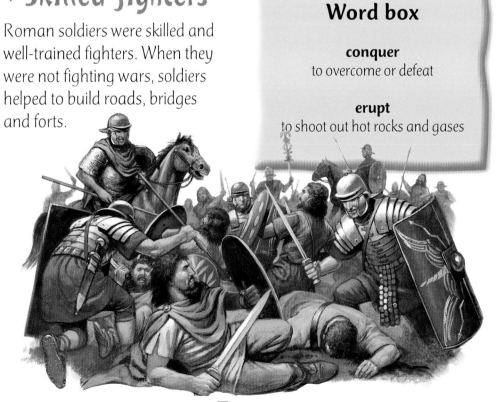

Science

Science is a way of understanding our world – by watching, examining, collecting information and carrying out experiments. Science involves the study of everything – from stars to skeletons, planets to plants, dinosaurs to diseases. There are many different areas of science. The science of biology, for example, looks at living things. Astronomy involves the study of the stars, planets and the entire Universe, while meteorology is the study of the weather.

▲ In the laboratory

Many scientists work in special places called laboratories. Here they carry out experiments, look at the results and try to put together new scientific ideas. Many new drugs to treat ill people are made and tested in scientific laboratories.

▼ Keeping records

Geology is the study of the Earth. This involves looking at rocks, earth, taking samples and monitoring volcanoes and earthquakes. These geologists are studying a nearby volcano.

Wow!

Isaac Newton made his discovery about a force called gravity when, in the 1600s, he saw an apple fall to the ground in an orchard.

▼ Freezing conditions

Scientific studies may involve working in extreme conditions. This means that being in the right surroundings, or environment, is very important. These scientists are taking temperature readings in the freezing conditions of the Antarctic.

Match the names

A biologist is a scientist who studies living things. Can you match each of these scientists with the things they study?

1. botanist
2. archaeologist
3. meteorologist
4. geologist
5. zoologist

a. animals
b. Earth
c. plants
d. historical places
e. weather

1c 2d 3e 4b 5a
answers

Scientists

Find out more:
Communication ◄ Electricity ◄ Greeks ◄ Lighting ◄
Science ◄

Scientists have developed many of the things we use every day – lightbulbs and lasers, plastics, televisions and telephones.
They also help us to understand how the world works – and how our own bodies work, too. Some scientists, such as the mathematician Albert Einstein (1879–1955), are famous around the world.

◄ Eureka!

A scientist called Archimedes lived in Greece over 2,000 years ago. He made some important discoveries in physics and mathematics. He made one discovery while in the bath. Archimedes is said to have jumped out of the bath and run into the street without any clothes, shouting the word 'Eureka!', which means 'I have found it!'.

◄ Important ideas

Isaac Newton was an English scientist who lived in the 1600s and early 1700s. He had many important ideas about light and colour, and about a pulling force called gravity. Newton realized that gravity keeps the Moon travelling on its path around the Earth.

Wow!

As a boy, Thomas Edison worked on a train, selling newspapers and sweets to the passengers. In his spare time he carried out chemical experiments in the train's luggage compartment.

▼ Edison's inventions

An American scientist called Thomas Edison (1847–1931) invented the electric lightbulb. In his laboratory he also invented the world's first record-player. Modern hi-fi players, tape recorders and video recorders are based on Edison's invention.

► Dangerous work

Marie Curie and her husband Pierre were scientists who worked in France in the late 1800s and early 1900s. Marie Curie was a clever and hard-working physicist who discovered a dangerous but useful chemical substance called radium.

Seashore life

Find out more:
Birds of the world ◄ Oceans and life ◄
Oceans and seas ◄

The seashore is the place where the water from an ocean or sea reaches the land. Some seashores are rocky places with colourful seaweeds and rockpools filled with crabs, shrimps and other sea creatures. Other seashores are covered with sand or mud, where crabs and small worms burrow beneath the soft, wet surface.

▼ Seashore life

The part of the seashore closest to the sea is wet for most of each day. Higher up the shore, it dries out when the tide goes out. The animals and plants that live on the seashore have to survive both wet and dry conditions.

oyster catcher

1. many seabirds build nests on high cliffs overlooking the shore. Some, such as the guillemot, never actually build a nest. Female guillemots lay eggs on narrow ledges

2. seabirds such as curlews and oystercatchers have long, pointed beaks. They use these to stab shellfish, tear open shells or find worms that burrow in the sand

curlew

3. small sea creatures such as shrimps and crabs hide in rockpools to avoid being eaten by hungry birds

shrimp

crab

Word box

anchor
to stop something from moving

burrow
to dig deeply

► In a rockpool

Rockpool creatures such as mussels and limpets cling to the rocks so they are not washed away by waves. Their shells protect them from the sea and the Sun.

4. seaweeds grow along the seashore. They have a special part that anchors them to the rocks. This is called a holdfast

limpet

mussel

Seasons

When each of the seasons arrives – spring, summer, autumn and winter – they bring changes with them. The weather and the temperature change, and days become longer or shorter. Some parts of the world have four seasons a year, others have only two – a wet and a dry season, or a dark and a light one.

▶ Moving Earth

The movement of the Earth around the Sun causes the seasons. As the Earth moves around the Sun, different places receive different amounts of sunshine because the Earth is tilted at an angle. For example, when the North Pole is tilted towards the Sun, places in the northern half (hemisphere) of the world have summer, while those in the southern half have winter.

2. in June the northern hemisphere is tilted towards the Sun

3. in September the northern and southern hemispheres receive equal amounts of Sun

1. in March the northern and southern hemispheres receive equal amounts of Sun

4. in December the southern hemisphere is tilted towards the Sun

▼ Hot places

The Equator is an imaginary line around the middle of the Earth. Places here are hot all year because the Sun shines directly above them. Rainfall in these places varies thoughout the year – a dry season is followed by a wet, stormy one.

▼ Harvest time

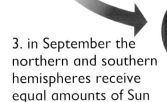

Grapes are ready to pick at the end of the summer. The harvest is usually good after a long period of dry, sunny weather.

Wow!

In places near the North Pole, the Sun shines for 24 hours a day during the middle of summer. This part of the world is called the 'Land of the Midnight Sun'.

▼ Winter and summer

These mountains in Switzerland are covered with snow in winter. During summer, cattle graze on the grassy slopes.

▲ Rainy season

In parts of Asia and Africa the rains are very heavy once a year. This is known as the monsoon season. It can cause floods, damage fields of crops and kill farm animals.

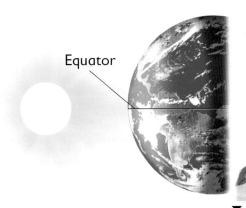

Equator

Ships and boats

Ships sail across open seas and lakes or travel along rivers and canals. They carry people and goods from place to place. Luxury ocean liners take thousands of passengers on holiday cruises. Giant oil tankers transport millions of tonnes of oil across rough seas. Cargo ships carry foods, cars and coal from one side of the world to the other.

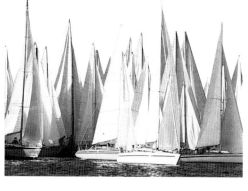

▲ Racing yachts

We sail yachts for pleasure and also for racing. Most yachts have one or more sails, but some have a motor engine only. Large racing yachts sail around the world with a crew of about 20 people on board.

◀ Small boats

A boat is a much smaller craft than a ship. Many boats have no engine and are propelled through the water by oars or sails.

▶ Sailing in style

The *Grand Princess*, built in 1998, is the second-largest passenger ship in service. It is second only to the *Voyager of the Seas*, launched in 2000. The *Grand Princess* is a huge, luxurious, floating hotel, weighing 109,000 tonnes. It has rooms for 2,600 passengers.

▼ Floating on air

A hovercraft is a ship that floats on a cushion of air. It can travel over land or water. Some hovercraft operate like car ferries and carry passengers and cars across water.

▼ Car ferries

Large ships called car ferries carry people and vehicles across small stretches of water. People drive their vehicles on and off through enormous doors at the bow (front) and stern (back) of the ferry.

Wow!
The largest tankers are over half a kilometre long. Sailors travel from one end of the tanker to the other by bicycle.

Ships in history

The first ships were either rafts made by tying logs together, or dugout canoes made from tree trunks. At first, boats were propelled by paddles, and then sails were added. Over 200 years ago came the invention of steam-powered boats. About this time, shipbuilders began to build iron ships instead of wooden ones.

▲ Reed boats

More than 5,000 years ago the Egyptians built lightweight river boats out of bundles of reeds. They were propelled by a long pole and, later on, by oars.

Word box

propelled
pushed forwards

propeller
a set of spinning blades that drives a ship

Greek cargo ship

◀ Strong and fast

The ancient Greeks built cargo ships which carried goods for trading. On the side of the ship were painted 'eyes'. The sailors believed these scared away evil spirits and protected them from harm.

SS Great Britain

◀ Fighting ships

Ships called galleons sailed the seas and oceans during the 1500s. They were used as fighting ships and to carry cargo. Galleons from Spain and England fought against each other in a famous sea battle off the south coast of England.

▲ Propeller power

The *SS Great Britain* was built in 1843. It was the first ship powered by a propeller to cross the Atlantic. The *SS Great Britain* was one of the first ships made of iron.

Wow!

Viking lords from northern Europe liked their warships so much that they asked to be buried inside them. They believed the ships would take them safely to the 'land of the dead'.

Sound

We hear sound all the time – from a ticking clock and a singing bird to a ringing doorbell or a car in the street.

Concorde

Every sound is made in the same way. An object shakes gently when it makes a noise. This shaking movement is called a vibration. The air around the object also starts to vibrate, and these vibrations travel through the air as waves of sound.

▲ At top speed

Sound travels through the air at about 340 metres per second. Sound waves travel more slowly than waves of light – light travels about one million times more quickly. Some jet aircraft travel faster than the speed of sound. When they do, they make a loud, booming noise.

◄ Bouncing waves

Bats produce high-pitched sounds that cannot be heard by humans or other animals. The sound waves bounce off the food they hunt, such as insects, then back to the bat, telling the bat where their food is.

sound wave bounces back to bat

bat

moth

sound wave from bat

oboe

► Speak up!

Our voices make sounds by vibrating our vocal cords. These are the soft flaps of skin in the voice box, at the back of the throat. When air passes over the vocal cords, they vibrate and make a sound. We then use our tongue and lips to change the sounds and form words.

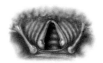

vocal cords are open and no sound is made

vocal cords close and air is forced out

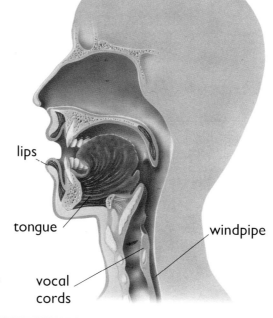

lips

tongue

windpipe

vocal cords

▲ Musical sounds

Musical sounds are made in many different ways. The sound from a guitar is made by plucking the strings, which start to vibrate. When a musician blows into an oboe or a flute, the air inside the instrument vibrates, creating sound. The skin across the top of a drum vibrates when it is hit with a drumstick or a hand.

Sound and hearing

Find out more:
Human body ◄ Music ◄ Sound ◄

The sounds you hear have travelled through the air and into your ears. They travel as invisible sound waves. As they enter your ears, the sound waves make your eardrums vibrate. These vibrations pass to nerves in your ears, which carry messages about the sounds to the brain. Your brain helps you to understand the different sounds you hear.

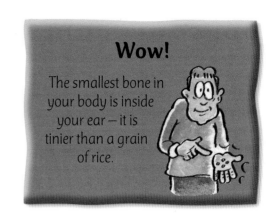

Wow!

The smallest bone in your body is inside your ear — it is tinier than a grain of rice.

► Into the ear

Your ear is divided into three main parts: the outer ear, which is the part you can see and touch, the middle ear and the inner ear. Your eardrum (a piece of flexible skin) separates your outer ear from your middle ear.

▼ Levels of sound

Sound is measured in units called decibels (dB). For example, a whisper measures only 20 decibels, while an atomic explosion measures 200 decibels.

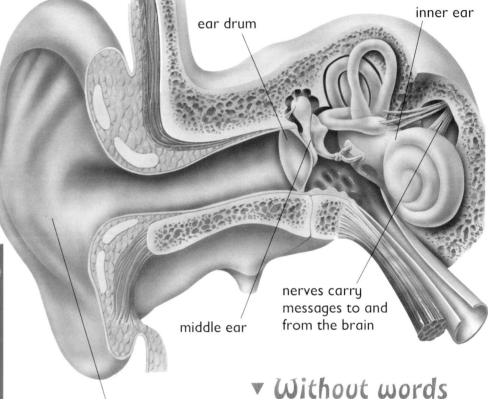

ear drum

inner ear

nerves carry messages to and from the brain

middle ear

outer ear

▼ Without words

Deaf people hear either faint sounds or no sounds at all. Many deaf people communicate with each other with the help of sign language. They use their hands, face and the top half of their body to make signs. Each sign has a different meaning.

On the move

You can listen to music on the move with the help of a small personal stereo. If you listen to very loud music too often, you may damage your ears.

Word box

atomic
to do with atoms, the smallest parts of anything

nerve
a tiny thread that carries messages to the brain

South America

Find out more:
Mountains ◄ Rainforests ◄ Rivers and lakes ◄
South America and its people ►

South America is the fourth biggest continent in the world. You can find almost every kind of land feature there. South America has hot, steamy rainforests and dry deserts, towering, snow-capped mountain peaks and wide, grassy plains, active volcanoes and spectacular waterfalls. By far the biggest country in South America is Brazil, which covers almost half of the continent.

► Copper mines

South America has large amounts of valuable minerals such as gold, copper and lead. Some of the world's biggest copper mines are in Chile. Miners remove the copper from underground mines or huge open pits on the surface.

► High and low

High up among the jagged peaks of the Andes Mountains rise the snow-covered tips of active volcanoes, such as Cotopaxi. This volcano, which is in Ecuador, has erupted over 25 times during the past 400 years.

▼ Full of life

In the basin of the Amazon river lies the Amazon rainforest, the largest in the world. It contains more kinds of plants and animals than any other forest.

parrot
jaguar
snakes
toucan
monkey

Word box

basin
the area where a river collects its water

jagged
sharp and pointed

mineral
tiny pieces of rock

South America and its people

Find out more:
South America ◄

About three-quarters of all South Americans live in cities and towns. **Many poor people leave the countryside to look for work in the city. They often earn very little money and live in 'shanty' homes with no electricity or running water. There are groups of Native Americans, such as the Aymara of Bolivia and the Guarani of Brazil, in most countries. These peoples lived in South America before the settlers arrived from Europe.**

Word box

native
someone born in a particular place

network
something that is linked,
like a series of roads

▲ Old traditions

The Aymara Indians of Bolivia speak their own language and follow a traditional way of life. Most are farmers, but they also weave textiles, build reed boats and make pottery to earn money.

▶ Big cities

Cities like Brazil's São Paulo (right) and Rio de Janeiro are growing quickly. São Paulo has towering skyscrapers and busy streets. However, there are not enough houses, and many people live in poor areas called shanty towns.

▲ Conquerors from Europe

In the 1500s, soldiers from Spain and Portugal came to South America to conquer the peoples living there. They took over their lands and riches. The Europeans were attracted by the gold they saw. They also wanted to teach the Christian religion to the people.

▼ Great builders

The Inca people ruled large areas of South America in the 1400s and 1500s. These great builders made a network of roads across the Andes Mountains. The walled city of Machu Picchu, now in ruins, was built by the Incas in Peru.

Machu Picchu

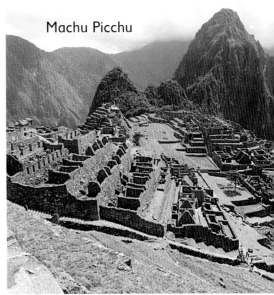

Where am I?

Solve this riddle to find the name of a South American country.
My first is in COUGH but not in BOUGH.
My second is in THEE but not in TEE.
My third is in PIG but not in PUG.
My fourth is in TALE but not in TEA.
My last is in SEW but not in SOW.

answer
CHILE

Space travel

Find out more:

Moon ◀ Planets ◀ Spacecraft ▶

The first person to travel in space was a Russian called Yuri Gagarin. In 1961 he circled the Earth for about 90 minutes in a tiny *Vostok* spacecraft.

Eight years later, the first men walked on the surface of the Moon. Since then, astronauts have walked in space, repaired telescopes in space and lived for months at a time inside space stations.

Yuri Gagarin

▼ Space dog

A dog named Laika was the first living thing to go into space. In 1957 she travelled in a Russian spacecraft called *Sputnik 2*, and stayed in space for two weeks.

▲ Protective suits

This astronaut is walking in space. His extra-thick suit protects him from any dangerous rays in space. A safety line attaches the astronaut to his spacecraft.

Word box

astronaut
a space traveller

cosmonaut
a Russian space traveller

Wow!

A Russian cosmonaut spent 438 days in space inside the *Mir* space station.

▼ To the Moon

Three American astronauts flew to the Moon in the *Apollo 11* spacecraft. While one astronaut stayed in the main spacecraft, the others landed on the Moon in a smaller vehicle.

rocket

Apollo 11 command module

lunar module

◀ Visiting crews

The American *Skylab* was launched in 1973. It was the second space station to be launched, beaten by the Russian *Salyut 1* in 1971. Despite a few problems, three 3-man crews visited *Skylab* and the longest mission lasted 84 days. The 75-tonne space station eventually burned up in the atmosphere in 1979.

Spacecraft

Find out more:
Communication ◀ Planets ◀ Space travel ◀

Spacecraft have travelled enormous distances through space to visit all the planets, except Pluto. No human beings have landed on any of the planets yet. The first spacecraft were tiny capsules with no one on board. Astronauts now travel into space in a space shuttle. This spacecraft, which can be used again and again, lands back on Earth like an aircraft.

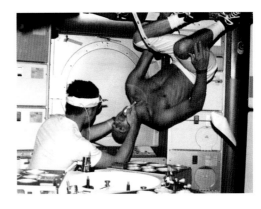

▲ Living in space

Astronauts can live and work inside a space station for more than a year at a time. They have their own supplies of air, food and water. The astronauts carry out experiments in the special conditions of space. Spacecraft from Earth bring fresh supplies to the space station.

◀ Satellite in space

A satellite is an object that circles the Earth, up in space. Hundreds of satellites have been placed in space by scientists to send radio, TV and telephone signals around the world. *Sputnik 1*, the very first spacecraft, was a satellite. It was launched by the Russians in 1957.

▼ Rocket power

The *Ariane* space rocket lifts off into space in a cloud of fire and hot gases. It launches satellites for European countries. The letters 'ESA' on the side of the rocket stand for European Space Agency.

▲ Space station

A number of countries have joined together to build a huge new station in space called the International Space Station, or ISS. Some sections of the station have already been built and taken into space. The station will begin working in 2002.

Wow!

The USA's two unmanned *Voyager* spacecraft carry recorded messages from people on Earth. This is in case they meet any other living things in space.

▼ Back to Earth

The USA's space shuttle is launched into space by a huge rocket, but it lands back on the ground along a runway. A parachute at the back helps it to slow down after landing.

Spiders

Find out more:
Animal kingdom ◀ Insects ◀
Spiders and their relatives ▶

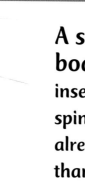

A spider is a creature with eight legs and a body divided into two main parts. Spiders are not insects, although many people think they are. Most spiders spin webs, which they use to trap their prey. Scientists already know of more than 30,000 different kinds of spider.

▼ Catching food

Spiders have a number of ways of catching their food. Bolas spiders catch insects on a silky thread with a sticky ball on one end. House spiders trap flying insects in their silky webs. Wolf spiders are fast runners that chase after their prey.

▲ Wonderful webs

Spiders spin webs in many shapes and styles. House spiders spin a tangle of silky threads attached to a wall or ceiling. Black and yellow garden spiders spin beautiful round webs with a zigzag of silk across the centre.

wolf spider

▲ Hairy spiders

Hairy spiders called tarantulas are the biggest spiders of all. Some can even eat small animals such as birds, frogs and mice.

spiderling

Wow!

The water spider lives in a bell-shaped nest that it builds underwater.

▶ Baby spiders

A mother spider, like the black widow shown here, can lay hundreds of eggs. The eggs are left inside a silky bag. The eggs hatch when the weather becomes warm. The newly hatched spiders are called spiderlings.

Spiders and their relatives

Find out more:
Animal kingdom ◄
Insects ◄ Spiders ◄

Spiders belong to a group of animals called arachnids. This group also includes scorpions, harvestmen and mites. Unlike insects, arachnids have no wings. They have four pairs of legs while insects have three. Spiders and scorpions are thought of as scary, but most do not harm humans. Mites burrow under skin, making it sore and itchy. Some pass on disease.

poisonous sting

leg

external skeleton

pincer (claw)

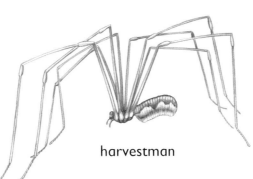

◄ Stinging tail

Scorpions live in warm places. They hide in the day and come out to hunt for food at night. A scorpion has a curved sting at the end of its long tail. It uses the poison in this sting to kill its prey. A scorpion sting is painful for humans but it does not usually cause death.

▼ Blood suckers

Ticks are small egg-shaped animals, and are a type of mite. They live on the bodies of other animals and feed by sucking their blood. Ticks are dangerous because they pass diseases into the blood of their victims.

this image has been magnified to show close-up detail of a tick

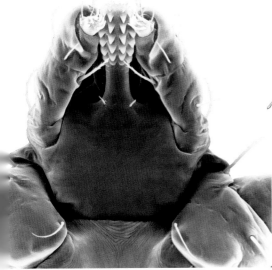

▲ Baby scorpions

Scorpions do not lay eggs – they give birth to live, fully formed young. The young hang onto their mother's back for the first two weeks after they are born.

harvestman

▲ Very long legs

The long-legged harvestman is a harmless creature. It eats small insects and fruit that it finds on the ground. Another name for it is daddy longlegs.

Wow!

Female ticks can lay as many as 18,000 eggs at a time.

Sport

Find out more:
Bicycles ◄ North American life ◄ Oceania and its people ◄
Sporting events ►

Sport provides entertainment for millions of people. Some sports involve individuals, others involve entire teams. Sport can also help to keep us fit. Many people play sport just for fun, but for others, it is their job. Great numbers of people watch athletes at stadiums (huge sports grounds), or follow them on TV or radio.

▼ In the basket

Basketball is played by two teams of five players each. It is the most popular indoor sport. A Canadian teacher invented the game in 1891 to keep his students busy during the long, dark winters.

▼ Up in the sky

Skydiving involves jumping from an aircraft and performing special moves in the air. Skydivers wear parachutes that help them to land safely on the ground. Teams of skydivers sometimes join hands in the air before their parachutes open up.

▲ Most popular

Soccer is probably the world's most popular sport. Top soccer teams play matches in stadiums in front of thousands of fans. The first rules for the game were drawn up in England in the 1800s.

▼ Steering through the water

Windsurfing is a very popular water sport even though it only started about 40 years ago. The windsurfer must balance on a sailboard while steering it through the water at top speed.

Wow!

Each American football team has around 45 players but only 11 are allowed onto the pitch at one time.

Sporting events

A top sporting competition is a major event. For example, the Wimbledon tennis tournament is held each summer in London. Every four years, soccer's World Cup takes place. The world's biggest sporting event is the Olympic Games. This also occurs every four years and features a huge variety of sports. People come from all over the world to represent their countries.

Pete Sampras has won Wimbledon a record seven times

▲ World class

The best tennis players can earn millions of pounds. They receive prize money when they win a competition. World-class players also receive money from the sports companies whose clothing and equipment they wear and use.

► Hard work

Gymnasts have to train very hard to be able to perform in national and international competitions. The very first gymnasts were soldiers in ancient Greece.

▲ Winter sports

The most important competition for winter sports is the Winter Olympic Games, which takes place every four years. The main sports held are skiing (above), ski jumping, skating and bobsleigh racing.

▼ Game of patience

At the world chess championships millions of people follow every move of the champion players. Chess is a board game that is played by two players. It is a game of skill and patience. The winner is the one who traps the main piece, the king, of the other player.

▼ Motor racing

Large numbers of people watch motor racing, either at a circuit or on the television. The fastest cars are called Formula One cars. They take part in about 17 races around the world each year, to find the best driver and the best make of car.

Wow!

A bobsleigh can travel at over 130 kilometres an hour along a track made of of solid ice.

Stars

Have you ever seen stars twinkling?
These stars are part of the Milky Way galaxy,
the family of stars that surrounds our planet.
Light from faraway stars takes years
to reach Earth. Light from our nearest
star, the Sun, takes eight minutes
to reach us.

▼ Star patterns

Patterns formed by stars are called
constellations. Many are named
after animals and people from
Greek myths. The constellation of
Orion is named after Orion the
Hunter. A row of three stars
across the middle makes up the
hunter's belt.

Milky Way

Hubble Space Telescope

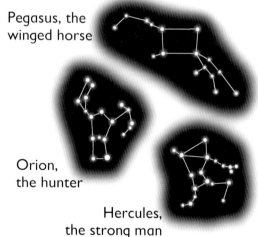

Pegasus, the
winged horse

Orion,
the hunter

Hercules,
the strong man

▶ Star-watching

People who study stars and planets
are called astronomers. Modern
astronomers use very powerful
telescopes. Some telescopes have
been placed in space. They send
pictures back to Earth. The most
famous of these is the Hubble
Space Telescope.

▼ Life and death

New stars are born all the time –
and old ones die. New stars are
born inside clouds of dust and gas.
Large stars swell before they die.
Then they
disappear
in a huge
explosion.

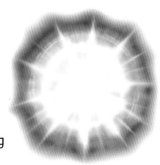

exploding
star

▼ Different stars

Stars give off heat and
light. A blue-white
star is very hot, but
a red coloured star is
cooler. Our Sun is
supergiant a main sequence star,
which means that it is
medium-hot.

main sequence star

Word box

constellation
a well-known pattern
of stars

galaxy
a huge family of stars

supergiant
a huge red star that is
beginning to cool down

Sun

The Sun is a huge ball of hot, glowing gas. It provides the heat and light that living things on Earth need to stay alive. It is our nearest star, which is why it looks bigger than other stars. The Sun is about 50,000,000 kilometres from the Earth.

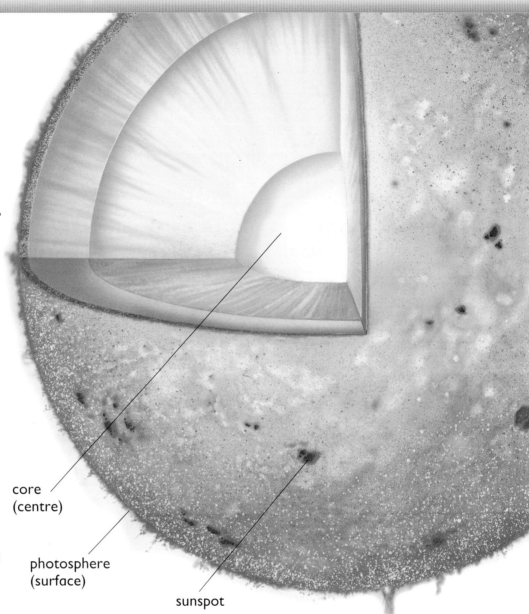

core
(centre)

photosphere
(surface)

sunspot

◄ Very hot

The Sun is very, very hot. The temperature on its surface is about 6,000 degrees Celsius — that's 60 times hotter than boiling water. The centre of the Sun is almost 3,000 times hotter than its surface.

▼ Spots and flares

Dark spots sometimes appear on the Sun's surface. These are called sunspots. The Sun can give off huge bursts of bright light called flares. They shoot out from its surface.

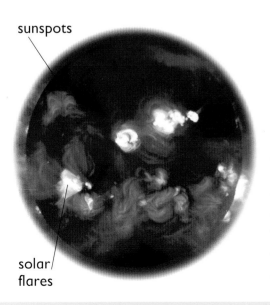

sunspots

solar
flares

▲ Telling the time

You can use the Sun to tell the time. A sundial is a kind of clock that shows how a shadow changes as the Sun moves across the sky. You tell the time by looking to see where the shadow falls on the dial.

▼ Sun worship

People worshipped the Sun long ago. The ancient Egyptians and Greeks believed the Sun was a god. The Aztecs of Central America built pyramids to honour the Sun.

Aztec pyramid

Television and films

Find out more:
Communication ◄

Television brings many kinds of event into right into our homes. These include news from around the world, sport, music, wildlife programmes, action films and children's cartoons. In the world's wealthier countries, almost every home has a television set.

◄ Early TV

Scottish engineer John Logie Baird developed an early form of TV in the 1920s and 1930s. This system used lenses set into revolving discs.

▼ In the studio

This picture shows newsreaders being filmed inside a TV studio as they read the news. Other parts of the news programme are filmed 'on location' – out and about wherever the story takes place.

► Making pictures

Television programmes are sent to your home by radio waves. The aerial on your roof picks up these waves and converts them into electrical signals. Your television changes these signals into pictures and sound using electron guns and beams.

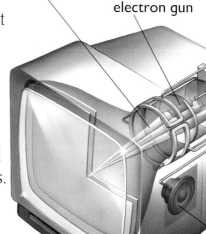

electron beam

electron gun

outside aerial

loud speaker

screen

▼ Making films

The films we enjoy on TV and at the cinema often take many months to make and cost large amounts of money. As well as actors, many other people are involved in a big film, from the overall director to the camera crew and make-up artists.

Theatre

Find out more:
Greeks ◄

People go to the theatre to watch a play, a musical show, an opera or a ballet. The performance usually takes place on a stage at the front of the theatre. The audience sits in rows facing the stage. Thousands of years ago, plays were performed in open-air theatres in ancient Greece.

Wow!

In the 1500s, if an audience disliked the play they shouted out rude remarks and threw rotten vegetables at the actors.

► In ancient Rome

Roman theatres were huge, well-built structures. One of the best-preserved is at Orange, in France. It has seats for almost 10,000 people. It was so cleverly designed that the audience could hear the actors, even from the back row.

scenery could be complicated, so it was moved around by machinery.

stage

▼ Famous writer

William Shakespeare (1564–1616) was a successful English playwright (a person who writes plays) who lived during the reign of Queen Elizabeth I. Many of his plays were performed at Elizabeth's court. Today, Shakespeare is still one of the world's best-known writers.

► The Globe

The plays of William Shakespeare were performed in London's Globe Theatre in the 1600s. An exact copy of the original theatre close to the same site was completed in 1996.

▲ Modern theatre

Many new theatres are modern-looking buildings, like the National Theatre in Ghana, Africa.

Time

We need to know the time throughout each day – to get up in the morning, to catch the school bus, to find out what time a television programme starts. We measure time by counting the seconds, minutes and hours of each day, as well as the weeks and months of each year.

▶ First calendars

Calendars help to keep track of days, weeks, months and years. The Mayan people of central America made a stone calendar on the ground, in the shape of the Sun. The face of the Sun god was carved in the middle and signs for the days carved around the outside. Time was tracked by the Sun's movement.

digital clock

◀ Old and new

Modern digital clocks tell you the time by simply displaying numbers. Older-style clocks have round faces with the numbers 1 to 12 around the edge. Two hands move round and point to the correct time.

▲ Night and day

People on opposite sides of the world have day and night at different times. As the Earth spins round, half the world is in daylight and the other half faces away from the Sun and has night. When it is 11 o'clock in the morning in London, UK, the time in Sydney, Australia is 9 o'clock at night.

▶ Very accurate

Scientists keep time with special atomic clocks. These are much more accurate than ordinary clocks. They keep time by measuring how fast an atom (a tiny particle of matter) vibrates.

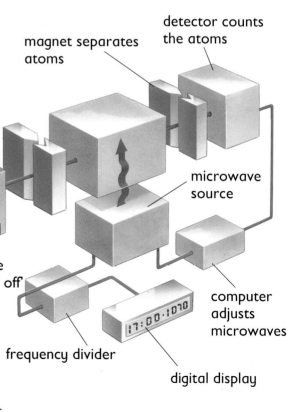

magnet separates atoms

detector counts the atoms

microwave source

oven where atoms 'boil off'

frequency divider

computer adjusts microwaves

digital display

Word box

accurate
correct

frequency
the number of radio waves per second of a radio signal

Towns and cities

Find out more:
Buildings ◄ Homes ◄

Towns and cities are noisy, bustling places where lots of people live. Their streets are usually filled with buses, cars and taxis, and their pavements are packed with people. Many people work in towns and cities – in offices and shops, workshops and factories. Cities are bigger places than towns, and have more inhabitants.

Word box

inhabitant
someone who lives in a place

spire
a tall, pointed tower on top of a building

▼ Rush hours

Every morning, city streets are filled with people going to work. They flood into cities from surrounding areas and nearby towns and villages. They travel by car, bus and train. Each evening they go home again. We call these busy times rush hours.

► Ancient spires

The historic city of Oxford has many beautiful, old buildings and graceful spires. It is the home of England's oldest university. The first students came to the city around the 1100s.

▲ Modern and old

The city of Tel Aviv in Israel stretches as far as the eye can see. It is Israel's second largest city, and has some very modern areas. Cafés and fashionable shops can be found with parts of the city that date back to Biblical times.

▼ Meeting place

The central meeting place in many towns is the town square, like this one in the Greek town of Rhodes. Busy markets are often held each week in the town square.

Match the names

Can you match each of these capital cities with its correct country?

1. BEIJING   a. INDIA
2. PARIS   b. USA
3. NEW DELHI   c. EGYPT
4. WASHINGTON   d. FRANCE
5. CAIRO   e. CHINA

1e 2d 3a 4b 5c
answers

▲ New capital city

Canberra is the capital city of Australia. Unlike other capital cities around the world, Canberra is not an old or large city. It was specially built as a capital in the early 1900s.

Trains

Trains carry passengers and heavy loads along thick, metal tracks called rails. Passenger trains carry people on long journeys across a country or on short journeys to and from work. Some passenger trains in countries such as France and Japan travel at very fast speeds. Goods trains carry heavy loads such as coal, timber and chemicals.

► High speed

Japan's high-speed passenger train is known as the 'bullet train'. It can travel at speeds of up to 260 kilometres per hour.

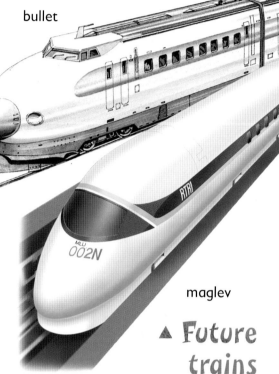

bullet

maglev

◄ By steam

Once, all trains were steam-powered. The steam was produced by burning coal to heat water in big boilers. Some countries still have steam trains. Most modern trains run on electricity or diesel fuel.

▼ Underwater

The Channel Tunnel, which links England and France, was opened in 1994. The rail tunnels are 50 kilometres long and were built at a depth of 37 metres under the sea. The train journey through the tunnels takes just 35 minutes.

▼ Underground

In some big cities, underground trains travel along rails in tunnels built beneath city streets. The world's first underground system was opened in London in the 1860s.

▲ Future trains

The maglev train is suspended by powerful magnets above a track. It can reach speeds of 400 kilometres per hour!

Wow!

The city of New York, USA has 466 underground railway stations — that's more than any other city in the world.

Trees

Find out more:
Air ◄ Forests ◄ Materials ◄ Plants ◄
Plants around the world ◄ Rainforests ◄

Trees are the largest plants of all. The biggest tree alive today, a giant sequoia in California, USA, is over 80 metres tall. Trees provide us with wood for building and to make paper. They give us fruits such as oranges and apples, and important materials such as rubber and cork. Trees also take in carbon dioxide from the air, and give off oxygen, the gas needed by all living things.

▼ Trees in blossom

Blossom is the name for the sweet-smelling flowers of some trees. The flowers then turn into fruit that we pick to eat. Inside are seeds from which new trees can be grown.

apple blossom on an apple tree

◄ Falling leaves

These are leaves from the North American maple tree. It is a deciduous tree, which means it loses its leaves each year and is bare in winter. Its leaves are green in spring and summer and turn gold, red and brown in autumn as they fall to the ground.

▼ Evergreen trees

Non-deciduous trees are called evergreens – they keep their leaves all year round. Some evergreens, such as pines, have needle-like leaves and woody cones. The seeds from which new trees will grow develop inside these cones.

▼ Inside the trunk

A rough, woody layer called bark protects the living parts of the tree beneath. Each year the sapwood beneath the bark grows, leaving a ring. This is how the age of fallen or damaged trees can be determined. Each ring is equivalent to one year.

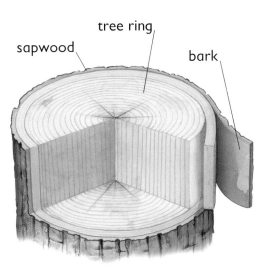

sapwood

tree ring

bark

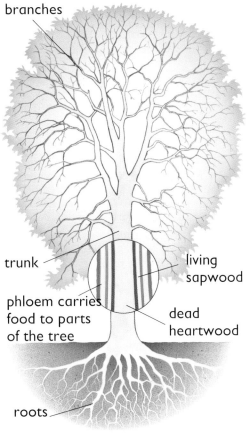

branches

trunk

phloem carries food to parts of the tree

living sapwood

dead heartwood

roots

◄ Parts of a tree

A tree has three main parts: the trunk and branches, the leaves and the roots. The branches and leaves together are called the 'crown'. The trunk supports the crown. The roots are underground and they absorb water from the soil.

Universe

Find out more:
Earth ◄ Planets ◄ Space travel ◄ Stars ◄

The Universe is everything that exists. It includes the Earth and the other planets, millions and millions of stars and everything else as far as the deepest corners of space. With the help of very powerful telescopes, scientists can now see far into the depths of the Universe.

▲ Deep space

The Hubble Space Telescope took this photograph of deep space. This telescope is high up above the Earth. It has sent back very clear and detailed pictures of parts of the Universe that we have never seen.

1. the Big Bang was a massive explosion that created the Universe

2. millions of years later, gases clustered into clouds

3. the clouds clumped together to form galaxies

4. millions of stars can be seen in the night sky, but these are just a tiny part of the Universe

Word box

clustered
grew close together

explosion
a very loud bang

▼ Studying stars

Astronomers are scientists who study planets, galaxies and other parts of space. They work in buildings called observatories where they use telescopes and other equipment. Observatories are often built on mountain tops, where the air is clearer. This gives a better view when looking through telescopes.

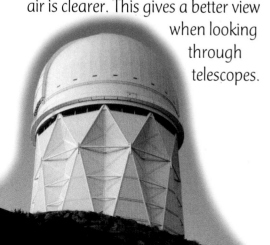

► How old?

The Universe is about 15,000 million years old. But how did it begin? It was probably born after a very large explosion. Scientists call this explosion the Big Bang. At first, the Universe was tiny, but then it grew bigger and bigger. It is still getting bigger today.

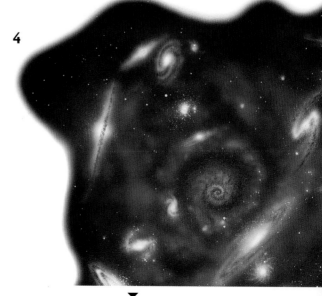

Volcanoes

Find out more:
Earth features ◄ Oceania ◄ Romans ◄ South America ◄

A volcano is an opening on the surface of the Earth. Most volcanoes are cone-shaped mountains. An erupting volcano is a spectacular sight. Red-hot liquid rocks pour out of the volcano's top and down its sides, thick clouds of gases and ash rise into the air and lumps of hot rock are blasted out.

Wow!

The biggest volcano disaster in recent times was an eruption of Mount Tambora in Indonesia in 1815 – it killed almost 100,000 people.

▼ Clouds of smoke

Thick clouds of smoke, hot gases and ash stream out of this volcano. Some volcanic clouds are so thick that they block out the Sun's light. When the ash reaches the ground it covers everything around the volcano in a grey blanket of dust.

▲ A new island

This is the island of Surtsey, in Iceland. It is named after Iceland's god of fire. This is because the island first appeared in the sea when a volcano erupted on the sea-bed in 1963.

▲ Red hot lava

The fiery red liquid that pours out of an erupting volcano is called lava. It comes from deep inside the Earth. When this hot liquid cools down, it hardens and turns into dark-coloured rock.

▶ Inside a volcano

The red-hot lava travels up through a pipe in the middle of the volcano. It pours out through the vent, the opening at the top of the volcano. Some of the hot lava leaks out through other openings in the volcano's sides.

▲ Good for growth

The soil around some volcanoes is full of nourishing substances which are good for plant growth. On the Italian island of Sicily, olive and lemon trees grow well at the foot of Mount Etna, an active volcano.

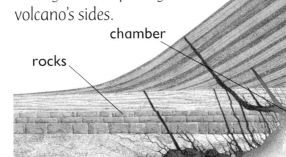

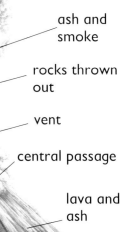

ash and smoke

rocks thrown out

vent

central passage

lava and ash

chamber

rocks

Water

Find out more:
Deserts ◄ Rivers and lakes ◄ Oceans and life ◄
Oceans and seas ◄ Weather ►

Water fills the Earth's oceans and seas and its rivers and lakes. Water is also found in the sheets of ice around the North and South Poles. It would be impossible to live on the Earth without water – all animals and plants need it to survive.

Wow!

You use about 10 litres of water every time you flush a toilet.

► Round and round

Water moves around our world in a continuous circle called the water cycle. During this cycle, water falls to the ground as rain and snow, returns to the air from the sea and the land and then falls back to the ground as rain and snow again.

water vapour cools, forming water droplets

plants give off water

water droplets fall as rain or snow

sea water evaporates

rivers carry water to the sea

► Collecting water

In poorer countries, many people have no running water in their homes. Instead they collect water from a well or stream in their village. Some people have to walk a long way to collect their water. They carry it back home in pots and other containers.

▼ Water at home

We use water in our homes for washing, cooking and cleaning. Water comes into our homes through pipes underground. Drains take away the dirty water.

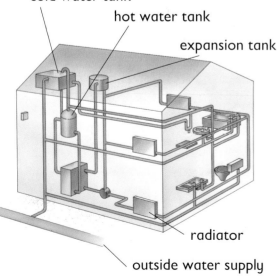

cold water tank

hot water tank

expansion tank

radiator

outside water supply

▲ Lack of rain

Some parts of the world receive little or no rain each year. A long period without rain is called a drought. The ground becomes hard and cracks, and crops shrivel and die. Often there are food shortages during a drought.

▼ Flash floods

If very heavy rain falls in a short period of time, a river cannot always carry the water away quickly enough. When this happens, a mass of fast-moving water called a flash flood spills onto the land.

Weather

Sunshine and clouds, winds and storms, rain and snow, frost and ice – these are all different kinds of weather. When the weather is fine, the sun shines and the sky is clear. In stormy weather, dark clouds fill the sky, strong winds blow and rain falls. The weather affects the daily work of many people, from farmers and sailors to aircraft pilots and mountaineers.

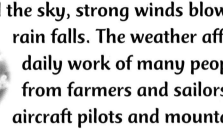

▲ Rain clouds

Drops of water fall from the clouds as rain. If the temperature inside a cloud is very cold, the water freezes and turns into hail or snow.

Word box

crystals
tiny six-sided pieces

isobar
line that connects places where air pressure is the same

predict
to say what will happen in the future

► Weather maps

Weather maps help us to predict what the weather for a particular area will be like. They are usually printed in newspapers and shown on television screens. Symbols on the map represent sunshine, rain, clouds, wind and other types of weather.

▲ Strong winds

A tornado is a windstorm that creates a huge funnel of whirling air. The tip of the funnel sucks up everything in its track. In the United States, tornadoes are called twisters. They can reach speeds of up to 50 kilometres an hour.

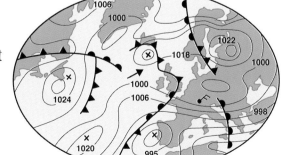

cold front

isobar

warm front

wind speed and cloud cover

▼ Farming

Farmers need to know what the weather ahead will be like. Their crops need the right amount of sunshine and rain to grow properly. Farmers like to harvest their crops in dry, sunny weather.

▼ Heavy snow

Snow is frozen crystals of water. Heavy snowfalls can cause a lot of damage and disruption. Snow may pull down electricity wires, delay trains and planes, damage plants and stop people travelling.

Word scramble

Unscramble these words to find five different weather terms

teles
renaceruh
inar
smort
smit

answers
sleet hurricane rain
storm mist

World

Find out more:
Africa ◄ Antarctica ◄ Asia ◄ Earth ◄ Europe ◄
North America ◄ Oceania ◄ South America ◄ Planets ◄

Our world consists of the planet Earth and all the living things on it. Millions and millions of people live here. The world's land areas are divided into almost 200 separate countries, and other areas that belong to certain countries. Each country has its own government and laws, and its own national flag.

▼ Big and small

The world's biggest country is Russia. It is millions of times bigger than the Vatican City, the smallest country in the world. The Vatican City lies in the Italian city of Rome.

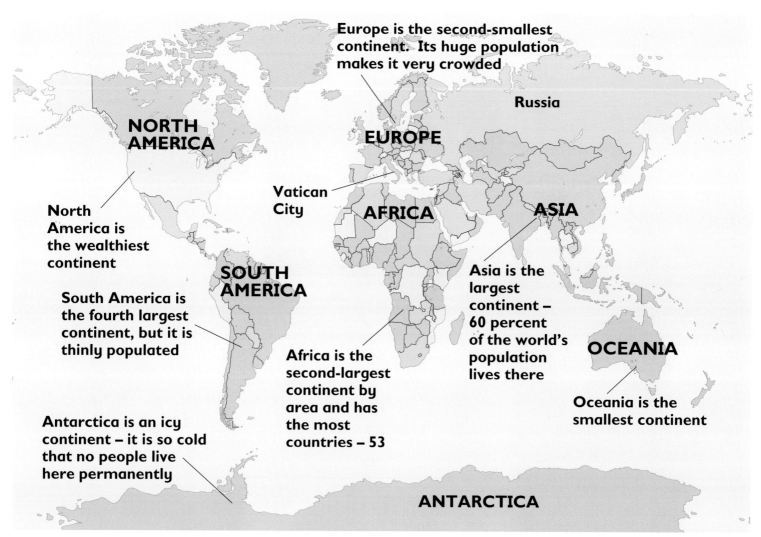

Europe is the second-smallest continent. Its huge population makes it very crowded

Russia

NORTH AMERICA

EUROPE

Vatican City

North America is the wealthiest continent

AFRICA

ASIA

SOUTH AMERICA

South America is the fourth largest continent, but it is thinly populated

Asia is the largest continent – 60 percent of the world's population lives there

OCEANIA

Africa is the second-largest continent by area and has the most countries – 53

Oceania is the smallest continent

Antarctica is an icy continent – it is so cold that no people live here permanently

ANTARCTICA

► United Nations

Wow!
Around the world people speak more than 3,000 different languages. The six most common ones are: Chinese, English, Spanish, Hindi, Arabic and Russian.

The United Nations is an organization that encourages peace between countries. Soldiers from member countries help to keep peace in troubled areas. The UN symbol shows a map of the world surrounded by olive branches, which traditionally stand for peace.

X-rays, Year, Zoo

Find out more:
Energy ◄ Human skeleton ◄ (X-rays)
Seasons ◄ Time ◄ (Year) Conservation ◄ (Zoo)

X-rays are a special kind of energy that moves in waves. X-rays are used to take pictures inside our bodies. These pictures help doctors and dentists to spot broken bones, check for disease and find out how healthy our teeth are. In industry, x-rays are used to find faults in machinery.

▼ Passing through

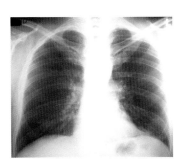

X-rays pass through the soft parts of the body, such as skin and muscles, but they are stopped by hard parts such as bones and teeth. This is an x-ray of the human rib cage.

the dragon marks the start of the New Year in China

▲ Chinese New Year

January marks the beginning of each year, but in many countries new year begins on a different date. The new year in China begins in February, while Jewish people celebrate the beginning of their year in September.

A year is the time it takes the Earth to travel around the Sun. A year lasts for 365 1/4 days. We add an extra day to every fourth year to have a year of 366 days. This means that the seasons always occur at the right time of year. Each year is divided into 12 months of either 28, 30 or 31 days.

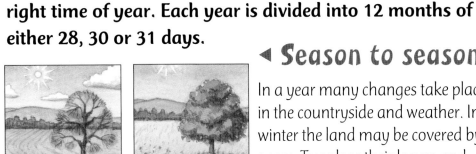

spring

summer

autumn

winter

◄ Season to season

In a year many changes take place in the countryside and weather. In winter the land may be covered by snow. Trees lose their leaves and some animals move to warmer places. In spring, the weather warms up, trees grow leaves, and animals give birth to young. Summer is warm, and flowers and fruit grow. In autumn, leaves turn brown and fall to the ground.

Animals from many different parts of the world are kept in zoos. The word 'zoo' is short for zoological gardens. Thousands of visitors come to a zoo to watch and study its animals.

◄ In the wild

Many zoos have helped to breed animals that are disappearing in the wild. When enough animals have been bred, some can be returned to the wild. Without this work, animals such as the Arabian oryx (left) and the European bison would have disappeared.

Index

The numbers in **bold** type refer to main entries in your book

**The publishers would like to thank
the following artists who have contributed
to this book:**

Lisa Alderson, Andy Beckett, Martin Camm,
Vanessa Card, Jim Channell, Kuo Kang Chen,
Mark Davis, Nicholas Forder, Mike Foster,
Terry Gabbey, Peter Gregory, Alan Hancocks,
Ron Haywood, Steve Hibbick, Rob Jakeway,
John James, Steve Kirk, Mick Loates, Kevin Madison,
Alan Male, Janos Marffy, Annabel Milne, Helen Parsley,
Jane Pickering, Gill Platt, Terry Riley, Andy Robinson,
Martin Sanders, Mike Saunders, Peter Sarson,
Guy Smith, Roger Smith, Sarah Smith, Mike Taylor,
Rudi Vizi, Gwen Tourret, Christian Webb, Mike White,
Paul Williams

**The publishers would like to thank Ted Smart
for the generous loan of his illustrations**

**The publishers would like to thank
the following for supplying photographs
for this book:**

Corbis: James L. Amos 70 (b/r); Yann Arthus-Bertrand
121 (t/r); Nathan Benn 86 (b/l); Bettmann 42 (t/r),
(c/r), 89 (c/l), 107 (t/r); Dean Conger 16 (b/r); Pablo
Corral 73 (b/r); Macduff Everton 114 (b); Natalie Fobes
58 (c/l), 79 (b/l); Marc Garanger 41 (c); Dave G.
Houser 31 (t/l); Craig Lovell 16 (c), 48 (c/r); Michael
Maslan Historic Photographs 66 (b/l); Stephanie Maze
31 (b/l); Amos Nachoum 76 (b/r); Clive Newton 124
(b/r); Chris North: Cordaiy Photo Library Ltd; 118(b/r);
Christine Osborne 73 (t/l), 76 (t/l); Charles O'Rear 104
(t/r); Roger Ressmeyer 104 (c), 121 (b/l); Reuters
NewMedia Inc 107 (b/l), 111 (t/l), (b/r); Lynda
Richardson 91 (t/c); Bob Rowan 22 (t/l); Joseph Sohm
17 (c/r); Alan Towse 10 (b/r); Bill Varie 58 (t/l); Ed Vashi
58 (t/r); Nik Wheeler 53 (c);
Adam Woolfitt 40 (b/r); Alison Wright 87 (b/l);
Tim Wright 114 (c/l) **Princess Cruises**: Grand Princess
100 (c) **Salter Housewares**: 68 (c/b)

All other pictures from the Miles Kelly Archives